Penguin Masterstudies

Joseph Andrews

David Nokes was educated at Christ's College, Cambridge, and now lectures in English at King's College, London. He is the editor of the Penguin Classics edition of Fielding's *Jonathan Wild* and author of *Jonathan Swift: A Hypocrite Reversed*, which won the James Tait Black Memorial Prize as the best biography published in 1985. In 1981 he wrote the BBC television biography of Swift, *No Country for Old Men*. At present he is writing a critical study of eighteenth-century satire and a television film on the education of the deaf in the eighteenth century.

Penguin Masterstudies
Advisory Editors:
Stephen Coote and Bryan Loughrey

Henry Fielding

Joseph Andrews

David Nokes

Penguin Books

Penguin Books Ltd, Harmondsworth, Middlesex, England
Viking Penguin Inc., 40 West 23rd Street, New York, New York 10010, U.S.A.
Penguin Books Australia Ltd, Ringwood, Victoria, Australia
Penguin Books Canada Limited, 2801 John Street, Markham, Ontario, Canada L3R 1B4
Penguin Books (N.Z.) Ltd, 182–190 Wairau Road, Auckland 10, New Zealand

First published 1987

Made and printed in Great Britain by
Richard Clay (The Chaucer Press) Ltd, Bungay, Suffolk
Filmset in Monophoto Times by
Northumberland Press Ltd, Gateshead, Tyne and Wear

For Tom, Moira, Ellie, Peter and Catherine

Contents

Introduction: The Rise of the Novel

The English have always favoured amateurs, and the emergence of the English novel in the eighteenth century is an episode to gladden the hearts of those who believe the best discoveries result from happy accidents, rather than from careful planning or large research grants. Daniel Defoe was almost sixty and nearing the end of a multifaceted career, during which he had been a merchant, spy, political agent, bankrupt and journalist, before he wrote the prose fictions for which he is now best remembered. Samuel Richardson was a successful printer, whose initial decision to try his hand at authorship may have derived as much from a thrifty resolve to exploit the spare capacity of his press as from any literary inspiration. Henry Fielding was enjoying a considerable reputation as a daring young playwright when Sir Robert Walpole imposed a new system of government censorship on stage plays and put an end to this phase of his career. None of these men had any pre-existing notion of what a novel *should* be. Indeed, only eight years before the publication of *Robinson Crusoe*, the *Tatler* was still using the word 'novelist' to mean a newspaperman. The traditions of the English novel then had their origins in a curious combination of journalistic opportunism, puritan enterprise and selective government censorship. The rich diversity of its subsequent development no doubt owes much to these heterodox beginnings.

In the view of Dr Johnson there was as great a difference between the literary talents of Samuel Richardson and Henry Fielding 'as between a man who knew how a watch was made, and a man who could tell the hour by looking on the dial-plate'. This notorious disparagement of Fielding's abilities has been answered by some equally forceful praise. Thackeray, who described Richardson's muse as being 'attended by old maids and dowagers, and fed on muffins and bohea', saluted Fielding's 'manly' virtues in these terms:

> He has an admirable natural love of truth, the keenest instinctive antipathy to hypocrisy, the happiest satirical gift of laughing it to scorn. His wit is wonderfully wise and detective; it flashes upon a rogue and lightens up a rascal like a policeman's lantern. He is one of the manliest and kindliest of human beings. (*The English Humorists of the Eighteenth Century*, 1853)

Though the terms of the judgements may vary, this temptation to draw comparisons between the literary achievements of Richardson and Fielding has persisted for over two centuries. For these two authors appear to embody two rival traditions of the English novel; they stand as contending 'fathers' of the novel, each disputing the legitimacy of the other's progeny. From Fielding we derive the rich tradition of comic fiction, a style of novel-writing that revels in its own exuberance and wit, and offers the reader a varied diet of social satire, moral example and verbal sophistication. But it is to Richardson that we owe the novel of moral introspection and psychological analysis, building a character from within and studying in depth the personal dramas of moral choice. One of the factors which gives *Joseph Andrews* its special significance and status in the history of the English novel is that not only is it Fielding's first attempt at the genre, but it also embodies his most serious critique of Richardson's fiction. It throws a bridge of comedy between the two traditions and offers a unique opportunity for a comparative evaluation of the qualities of both.

The mid-eighteenth century was a period when the established literary genres, such as poetry and the drama, were required at least to acknowledge, if not always to obey, the formal 'rules' of the ancients. Literary works were judged according to criteria enshrined in the writings of Aristotle and Horace, which laid particular emphasis upon unity of form, politeness of expression and decorum of manner. The novel, by contrast, enjoyed all the irresponsible freedom of a new and unclassified genre, and its practitioners were able to indulge a cheerful eclecticism of forms and content. Some, like Defoe, chose to call their works 'histories' or even 'true histories', and attempted, with varying degrees of seriousness, to pass them off as authentic chronicles of real events. Romances, on the other hand, exploited all the imaginative resources of fantasy to create a make-believe world of giants and dragons, enchanted isles and damsels in distress. In addition there were secret histories, like Mary Manley's *The New Atalantis*; travellers' tales, like *Robinson Crusoe*; moral allegories, like *The Pilgrim's Progress*; satires, like *Gulliver's Travels*; criminal lives, like *Moll Flanders*. Following the lapsing of the Licensing Act in 1695, there was an outpouring of, if not literary, at least printed artefacts of every conceivable shape, size, style, tone and genre to suit all tastes and pockets. Sermons and satires, pastorals and panegyrics, mingled with Grub Street fictions, newspapers and journals to meet the demands of a new middle-class readership unfamiliar and unconcerned with the strict criteria of neo-classicism. It was a period, laments Pope in the Introduction to *The Dunciad*, when 'paper became so cheap and printers so numerous that a deluge of authors covered the land'.

Fielding's greatest work, *Tom Jones*, is the story of a foundling, which is particularly apt since, as Pat Rogers observes, 'the early novel was genuinely regarded as a bastard among literary forms'. Joseph Andrews is a changeling, and that too is appropriate. For, in the Preface to *Joseph Andrews*, the narrator ostentatiously seeks to identify his new work with the classical tradition of Homer and Aristotle, and insists on dignifying it with the formal designation of a 'comic epic-poem in prose'. Although comic in tone, this description interestingly indicates something of Fielding's own ambivalence towards the novel form. In *The Rise of the Novel* Ian Watt criticizes an article by F. R. Leavis entitled 'The Novel as Dramatic Poem' as an apparent attempt 'to smuggle the novel into the critical Pantheon under the disguise of an ancient and honoured member'. Yet this is precisely what Fielding himself is doing with this mock-serious description. For, just as the characters Tom Jones and Joseph Andrews gain a knowledge of the world from their low-life adventures which will enhance their authority once they reassume their rightful place in polite society, so the novels which bear their name endeavour to revitalize classical forms and styles by a comic admixture of demotic caricature and satiric farce. Fielding's novels characteristically conclude with a reaffirmation of a traditional, hierarchical, Augustan view of the world. But his conservatism derives its confidence and vitality from the comic deployment of a 'common touch', mingling low-life escapades and real-life experiences with moral debates and traditional judgements.

Fielding's Early Career

Henry Fielding was born on 22 April 1707, probably at Sharpham Park in Somerset, and his family and forebears vividly exemplify the two sides of his nature. His mother's family, the Goulds, were sober, industrious gentry, and included two judges. But on his father's side the Feildings (so spelt) numbered in their ranks cavaliers, gamblers, rakes, soldiers, bigamists and duellists. Henry's mother died when he was just eleven years old and his father promptly remarried. Intense feuding between the Gould and Feilding sides of the family led to prolonged litigation, and Henry saw little of his father, who went on to a third, and possibly even a fourth marriage. Henry was dispatched to Eton College, where his fellow pupils included George Lyttleton, later the dedicatee of *Tom Jones*, William Pitt, later Prime Minister, and Thomas Arne, probably the leading British composer of the period. In Book III, Chapter 5 of *Joseph Andrews* Parson Adams and Joseph debate the relative merits of a public school education as against private tuition by a tutor. Adams is in no doubt about the matter. 'Public schools,' he declares, 'are the nurseries of all vice and immorality.' Joseph, on the other hand, sees the public schools as microcosms of the outside world, preparing the pupils in those worldly skills necessary to succeed in later life. Quoting his late master, Sir Thomas Booby, he asserts that 'a boy taken from a public school, and carried into the world, will learn more in one year there, than one of a private education will in five'.

Whatever Fielding's view of the matter, he certainly appears to have found the regime at Eton unpleasant, and is alleged to have run away at the age of fourteen. Four years later he attempted to elope with a fifteen-year-old heiress called Sarah Andrew. They ran away together to Lyme Regis, but their plans were foiled by Sarah's father, who hired some local thugs to thrash Fielding before having him bound over to keep the peace. At twenty Fielding wrote his first piece for the London stage; called *Love in Several Masques*, it combines some fictionalized episodes from his Lyme Regis escapade with dramatized echoes of Hogarth's satiric *Masquerades and Operas*.

Somewhat surprisingly, it was only after his first youthful success as a playwright that Fielding went to university, and then not to Oxford or Cambridge but to Leyden in the Netherlands. However, the lure of the stage was clearly stronger than that of study, for he returned to London in little over a year and set about establishing his career as a dramatist.

Between 1729 and 1737, while still in his twenties, Fielding became one of the capital's most prolific and successful playwrights. An item in the *Universal Spectator* for 1734 dubbed him 'Henry Drama' and remarked that he 'Brings on stage four pieces every season ... all wrote with uncommon rapidity.' The year 1731 witnessed a particular torrent of his youthful energies, and five new plays by him were performed at the theatre in Drury Lane. All sorts of dramatic works flowed from his pen: full-length comedies, farces, burlesques, afterpieces, prologues, epilogues, but above all ballad operas. The ballad opera was the latest craze, the newest theatrical fashion; it was introduced in 1728 (the year before Fielding's return to London) by the success of John Gay's *The Beggar's Opera*. The ballad opera combined the satirical sharpness of political cabaret with the sentimental melodies of a musical. *The Beggar's Opera* included satirical attacks on the political corruption of Sir Robert Walpole's Government, ironically comparing it with the protection rackets of the notorious underworld chief Jonathan Wild, who had been hanged in 1725. It also parodied the vogue for Italian opera, with allusions to the feuds and tantrums among leading castrati singers and prima donnas which had filled the gossip columns for several seasons. Yet these satirical touches were softened by being intermingled with charming sentimental ballads and traditional folk-songs like 'Over the Hills and Faraway' and 'Lilliburlero'. It was a formula which had an instant success, and *The Beggar's Opera* ran for an unprecedented sixty-two nights. The actress playing Polly Peachum, Lavinia Fenton, so charmed the Duke of Bolton, who came every night to watch her, that soon afterwards she became his duchess. There were *Beggar's Opera* playing-cards, fans, imitations and puppet-shows. This successful formula for combining topical satire with popular sentiment was an impresario's dream, and Fielding arrived in London just in time to exploit this new taste of the town.

An interesting point emerges when one examines Fielding's output as a dramatist in these early years. For all the varieties of composition which he attempted, his dramatic works can be roughly divided into two categories: full-length 'serious' comedies on the one hand and short burlesques, either farces or ballad operas (usually constructed on a 'rehearsal' model), on the other. Now the plain fact is that his burlesques, including such pieces as *Tom Thumb*, *Pasquin* and *The Historical Register for 1736*, are vastly more successful and enjoyable than his five-act comedies, such as *The Temple Beau*, *The Modern Husband* or *The Universal Gallant*. In his full-length plays Fielding's inventive talents seem inhibited and constrained by a conscious imitation of the epigrammatic style and formal structure of Molière or Congreve. *The Temple Beau* is a conventional comedy of manners and *The Modern Husband* is an unconvincing attempt at the style of sentimental comedy, but both are hampered by the same flaws: a weakness of plotting, a stiffness of language and a sense of padding to fill out the action to the appropriate length. Fielding takes no advantage of his extra space to develop the force of his characters, and there is little added depth to compensate for the lack of theatrical vitality and surprise.

In the burlesques, on the other hand, one recognizes Fielding's flair for technical daring and inventiveness, his instinct for theatrical improvisation. Though his characters have little depth, he deliberately revels in this two-dimensionality for a satiric effect, turning them into a kind of strip cartoon or political cabaret. The 'play-within-a-play' formula, a set-piece of Augustan satiric comedy from Buckingham's *The Rehearsal* to Sheridan's *The Critic*, provides each play with a running commentary from a group of critics and actors on stage. By this means theatrical parody and political satire are interwoven to demonstrate the affinities between the blank-verse bombast of heroic tragedies and the empty rhetoric of political speeches.

On the title pages of several of these plays Fielding called himself 'H. Scriblerus Secundus', thus proclaiming his allegiance to the values and standards of the Scriblerus Club, a group of satirists including Alexander Pope, John Gay and Jonathan Swift. The meetings of this club had taken place in the final months of Queen Anne's reign in 1714, but the main impact of Scriblerian satire had been delayed until the years just before Fielding himself began to write. The successive triumphs of *Gulliver's Travels* (1726), *The Beggar's Opera* (1728) and *The Dunciad* (1729) signalled a long-awaited challenge to the values of Hanoverian society. Fielding's early comedies demonstrate a clear indebtedness to the parodic and often surreal styles of Scriblerian satire. His mock-heroic play *Tom Thumb* (1730), revised and expanded the following year as *The Tragedy of Tragedies, or The Life and Death of Tom Thumb the Great*, is a kind of Lilliputian burlesque. The diminutive hero Tom Thumb, having single-handedly conquered a whole race of giants, falls in love with the giant princess Huncamunca. She, bewailing the cruel fates that have set obstacles in the path of their love, laments: 'O Tom Thumb, Tom Thumb, wherefore art thou Tom Thumb?' Audiences might naturally be expected to recognize this parody of Juliet's appeal to Romeo. However, the *cognoscenti* might realize that Fielding's real target is not Shakespeare but Otway's derivative and witless theft of the line in his tragedy *The History and Fall of Caius Marius*, where we find: 'Oh Marius, Marius, wherefore art thou Marius?'

At another climactic moment in *Tom Thumb* we witness a dispute between Grizzle and Noodle, two rival suitors for the princess's affections.

GRIZZLE: I will not hear one word but Huncamunca.
NOODLE: By this time she is married to Tom Thumb.
GRIZZLE: My Huncamunca?
NOODLE: Your Huncamunca? Tom Thumb's Huncamunca, everyman's Huncamunca.

The audience would hardly need to recognize the source of the parody here to experience a richly comic sense of burlesque. The princess's name is gross and vaguely suggestive, and the exchange has a kind of set-piece patter like the 'I say, I say' routine of a stand-up comedian. In fact, Fielding's target here too is another heroic adaptation of one of Shakespeare's plays, Dryden's *All for Love*.

ANTONY: What woman was it whom you heard and saw
        So playful with my friend? Not Cleopatra?
VENTIDIUS: Ev'n she, my lord.
ANTONY: My Cleopatra?
VENTIDIUS: Your Cleopatra,
        Dollabella's Cleopatra, everyman's Cleopatra.

At one level this is merely a delightful parody, the kind of situation comedy which Fielding excelled in creating. At another level, however, it represents a satiric attack on all false heroic postures, whether on stage or in politics. In Lilliput Swift reduces all struggles for political success to a farcical image of tiny courtiers dancing on a rope. In *The Beggar's Opera* Gay compares the Prime Minister to a gangland chief. In *The Dunciad* Pope's dunces debase the heroic motifs of Virgil's *Aeneid* to slapstick antics on the mudflats beside the Thames. What all these satires have in common is a kind of comic reductionism which transforms Olympian pretensions to the level of squabbles among insects. Heroic postures are reduced to farce, and high tragedy becomes low comedy. John Gay's burlesque comedy *The What D'Ye Call It* has the subtitle 'a tragi-comi-pastoral farce', which beautifully encapsulates the deliberate generic confusion created and exploited by the Scriblerian satirists. It was not that they disbelieved in the traditional literary forms or in the heroic virtues. On the contrary, it was the strength of their belief in classical values and traditions which drove them to expose and ridicule the tawdry travesties of modern imposters who sought to dignify their petty vanities with the trappings of classical iconography. For George II to usurp the mantle of Augustus Caesar, or for the Poet Laureate Colley Cibber to 'improve' Shakespeare, seemed clear indications of a society which had lost all true sense of value. The Scriblerians responded by creating a series of satires which deliberately conflated high and low, the sublime and the ridiculous.

The Scriblerians thus provided the inspiration for the inventive wit and ingenious parodies of Fielding's early plays. His burlesque comedies are full of youthful experimentation, politically provocative, theatrically adventurous, constantly taking risks. Above all he plays with all the conventional set-pieces of heroic drama, displaying a virtuosity which, if not always completely successful, exudes confidence and daring.

From 1734 till 1737 the Little Theatre in the Haymarket, where Fielding's 'Great Mogul's Company of Comedians' performed, acquired a reputation as the most daring anti-establishment theatre in town. But with the production of his three-act satirical comedy, *The Historical Register for 1736*, Fielding finally went too far for Walpole's patience. Within months the Licensing Act was passed, which required all theatres to hold a royal patent or special licence from the Lord Chamberlain. It further required all plays to be submitted to the Lord Chamberlain's office at least two weeks before performance, so that the text could be checked and censored. Though scholars now argue about Walpole's exact motives for passing this Act, which remained in effect until 1968, its effect was to put a sudden stop to Fielding's career. For seven years he had been working at building up a theatrical reputation which led Bernard Shaw to assert that Fielding was the best practising dramatist, apart from Shakespeare, between the middle ages and the nineteenth century (that is, until himself). Suddenly that star performance was cancelled by royal command, and Fielding's literary energies were diverted away from the stage and towards the novel.

Burlesque and Comedy

Ostensibly making light of this major stumbling block in his path, Fielding promptly turned his attention to the law and seems to have devoted the same impetuous energy to his legal studies that he had previously demonstrated as a dramatist. One biographer remarks on Fielding's capacity for combining bouts of concentrated study with occasional bursts of bohemian revelry. 'He has been frequently known, by his intimates, to retire late at night from a tavern to his chambers, and there read, and make extracts from, the most abstruse authors, for several hours before he went to bed.' Within three years Fielding had completed a course of studies which normally took six or seven, and was called to the bar in June 1740. No doubt the fact that he was now married with two small daughters added to the urgency of his desire to qualify himself for practice. For the next few years 'Counsellor Fielding' rode the Western circuit, taking in all the regular assize towns, such as Dorchester, Devizes, Salisbury, Taunton, Exeter and Bristol, familiarizing himself with the routes that his picaresque heroes, Tom Jones and Joseph Andrews, were to follow in his steps.

However assiduous his attention to the law, he had not entirely abandoned literary ambitions. While still a student at the Middle Temple he helped to produce a satirical paper called the *Champion* under the pseudonym of Captain Hercules Vinegar. Favourite targets for Vinegar's satire were Prime Minister Walpole and Poet Laureate Colley Cibber. In 1740 Cibber published his autobiography, *An Apology for the Life of Mr Colley Cibber, Comedian*, a gossipy, egocentric memoir, full of green-room scandal, chatty anecdotes and careless grammar. Fielding, seizing on Cibber's grammatical lapses, ridiculed the *Apology* – this 'suet-pudding' of a book – in a series of *Champion* papers. In one May issue he created a vivid court-room comedy, with Cibber arraigned before a Court of Censorial enquiry on a charge of murdering the English language. Despite the testimony of a number of witnesses, Cibber is finally convicted only of a 'chance-medley', a kind of manslaughter defined as 'homicide by misadventure'. His illiteracy, Fielding implies, is a matter of simple ignorance rather than conscious eccentricity.

Colley Cibber is probably best remembered now as the arch-dunce of Pope's final version of *The Dunciad* (1743). His combination of personal vanity with literary mediocrity made him an irresistible subject for Scriblerian satire. For Fielding too he remained a favourite target, and in both *Shamela* and *Joseph Andrews* one finds a number of sniping allusions to his *Apology*. However, it was another book published later that same year, 1740, which gave Fielding the real stimulus he required for the second phase of his literary career. In November the first part of Richardson's *Pamela* was published and had an immediate success. This impassioned and detailed first-person narrative of a young servant-girl's defence of her virtue against the lecherous designs of her employer was hailed as a triumph of the moral imagination. The *Weekly Miscellany* declared that it would 'reclaim the Vicious, and mend the Age in general'. Alexander Pope was entranced by the book which, he believed, would 'do more good than a great many of the new sermons'. A friend of Swift's went even further, declaring that 'if all the books in England were to be burnt, this book, next the Bible, ought to be preserved'. It was the fact that the book was both so moral and so real that gave it an enormous appeal. Unauthorized imitations and sequels quickly appeared, attempting to exploit the sudden *Pamela* vogue, even before Richardson could begin his own second part of the story. Yet, from the first, there were a few dissenting voices raised in criticism of the novel and its success. These tended to concentrate their attack on the materialistic implications of the novel's subtitle, 'Virtue Rewarded', seeing Pamela as a model of prudence rather than of purity. According to this view, the book's real moral represented a celebration of commercial self-interest rather than Christian ethics, since Pamela's defence of her virginity resulted in marriage and an enhanced social status which she could never have achieved as a mistress. Mrs Anna Barbauld, writing some years later, summed up this view when she said of Pamela: 'We can only consider her as the conscious possessor of a treasure, which she is wisely resolved not to part with but for its just price.' This was certainly the view adopted by Fielding, and his transformation of the virtuous Pamela into the cunning Miss Sham of *Shamela* underlines the point. In fact, those very qualities of dramatic realism which gave Richardson's first-person epistolary style its breathless immediacy also introduced elements of ironic humour into his heroine's character. His technique of writing-to-the-moment involves Pamela in a constant commentary on her own feelings which inevitably suggests a degree of self-consciousness at odds with her supposed innocence. Undoubtedly too there are some crudities of style in the book which produce an unintentional comedy that further undermines our belief in Pamela's innocence. Mark Kinkead-Weekes demonstrates one of these when he comments on the note of absent-minded surprise in Pamela's remark, 'I found his hand in my bosom.' As he writes, 'One has only to substitute the word "felt" to see the difference, for the odd tone is produced by the word that seems to make the bosom no part of the girl.' It is just such occasional dislocations of tone which Fielding exploits in *Shamela*, suggesting that this absent-mindedness may in fact be a cover for cunning, and that Pamela's vaunted 'modesty' may be no more than a subtle form of sexual teasing. One scene in *Shamela* beautifully counterfeits that combination of innocence and voyeurism that gives *Pamela* its ambivalent appeal.

THURSDAY NIGHT, TWELVE O'CLOCK

Mrs Jervis and I are just in bed, and the door unlocked; if my master should come – Odsbobs! I hear him just coming in at the door. You see I write in the present tense, as Parson Williams says. Well, he is in bed between us, we both shamming a sleep, he steals his hand into my bosom, which I, as if in my sleep, press close to me with mine, and then pretend to awake. – I no sooner see him, but I scream out to Mrs Jervis, she feigns likewise but just to come to herself; we both begin, she to becall, and I to bescratch very liberally.

Shamela is an accomplished and perceptive burlesque. Its techniques owe much to the style of theatrical parody demonstrated in *Tom Thumb* or *Pasquin*. Just as they parodied histrionic clichés and heroic pretensions, so *Shamela* ridicules the contrivances of the epistolary style and the prurient voyeurism lurking beneath Richardson's claims of moral purity.

Shamela was published in April 1741, only five months after the original *Pamela* and well before Richardson's own sequel. However, in the later months of 1741 Fielding was busily preparing a longer, more considered response to Richardson, and in February 1742 *Joseph Andrews* was published.

In the Preface to *Joseph Andrews* we find a careful distinction between comedy and burlesque. Indeed, Fielding's narrator goes so far as to assert, with considerable exaggeration, that 'no two species of writing can differ more widely than the comic and the burlesque'. Using his own terms, it is clear that *Shamela* is a burlesque 'where our delight . . . arises from the surprising absurdity' while *Joseph Andrews* is designed as a more dignified work of comedy, offering a 'just imitation' of nature. Yet as a playwright, as already noted, Fielding's genius lay in exploiting the surprising absurdities of mock-heroic parody and burlesque. His full-length comedies, by contrast, appear laboured, stiff and constrained. It is the remarkable achievement of *Joseph Andrews* that it marks Fielding's development from being a stage-manager of theatrical effects to becoming a mature comic artist.

In his study *Aspects of the Novel* E. M. Forster offers an observation whose seeming innocuousness conceals some dangerously misleading assumptions. 'The backbone of a novel,' he asserts, 'has to be a story.' While it may be true that most prose fictions contain some form of narrative or plot, this emphasis on 'story' represents a serious oversimplification of the possibilities available to fictional works. The 'story' contained in novels as widely separated in time as Sterne's *Tristram Shandy* and Virginia Woolf's *The Waves* would defy all attempts at narrative paraphrase, since these works deliberately challenge the linear representation of experience which a 'story' implies. Nor do such reservations about Forster's dictum apply only to the more experimental or eccentric forms of fiction. Samuel Johnson deplored the randomness and extravagance of *Tristram Shandy*, which he regarded as merely a form of ostentatious novelty. 'Nothing odd will do long,' he remarked, '*Tristram Shandy* did not last.' Yet Johnson was a sincere admirer of Richardson, whose novels, as he acknowledged, did not depend upon the subtlety of their stories for their success. 'If you were to read Richardson for the story, your impatience would be so much fretted that you would hang yourself. But you must read him for the sentiment, and consider the story as only giving occasion to the sentiment.'

What is true of Sterne and Richardson is also true of Fielding. Though the narrative structure of a novel such as *Joseph Andrews* demonstrates less obvious marks of originality than either *Tristram Shandy* or *Clarissa*, readers who approach it looking primarily for a good story involving realistic characters are likely to be disappointed. For a start, they are likely to be mystified and somewhat irritated by the narrator's habit of interrupting his tale with leisurely digressions, philosophical meditations and literary debates. They are likely to twirl over in impatience all the literary name-dropping on the first few pages where we find, in rapid succession, allusions to Cervantes, Homer, Aristotle, Fénelon, Shaftesbury, Ben Jonson, Colley Cibber and, of course, Samuel Richardson. They are likely to take the narrator at his word when he describes the digressions at the start of each book as 'inns or resting-places', natural breaks in the narrative flow, which serve no higher function than conveniently built-in book-marks. In other words, by reading *Joseph Andrews* simply in terms of its story one would risk ignoring all those counterindications of style, allusion, tone and narrative voice which remind us of the book's satiric context.

Readers in the eighteenth century were more accustomed to fictional works purveying a literary confection of story and commentary, narrative and digression, than we are today. Modern readers have, generally speaking, grown up with a novelistic tradition from Jane Austen to Graham Greene in which the story and characters are granted a kind of fictional integrity or autonomy of their own. Characters in such novels are not constantly subjected to digressions by the author, or elbowed aside to make room for an essay on etiquette, a satire on contemporary politics or a sermon on morality. The fictional tastes and expectations of readers in the eighteenth century were considerably more diverse. They had been shaped in part by such eccentric and protean works as Rabelais's *Gargantua* and *Pantagruel* and Swift's *A Tale of a Tub*, works which revel in their own literary eclecticism, gleefully combining elements of social satire, moral homily and narrative fantasy in an imaginative whole which defies easy categorization. In a similar fashion *Joseph Andrews*, with its digressions, doctrinal debates and interpolated tales, brings together a range of literary forms from *Spectator* essays to Hogarthian caricatures in a fictional structure whose main controlling device is not a story but the confident voice of the narrator.

As a satirical novel *Joseph Andrews* has inevitably something of a dual character, and the terms of that duality correspond in some ways to the distinction between burlesque and comedy already discussed. Unlike the novel, which is an autonomous entity that creates and sustains its own fictional world, satire always has its object and validation in external reality. Whereas a novel creates a network of relationships which are contained within itself, satire must always have an external reference to the society which produces it. Thus, in novelistic terms, Joseph Andrews is presented to us as the pupil of Parson Adams and the suitor of Fanny. But in the satiric structure of the work we recognize him as a parody of his virtuous 'sister' Pamela. On one level *Joseph Andrews* is a satire which ridicules Cibber and Richardson, and attacks venal judges and quack doctors. On another level it introduces a fictional world where innocence and good nature can triumph over hypocrisy and pride. It is important to keep both aspects of the book's character in mind as we investigate, in detail, its literary construction. Fielding's main fictional model, as he declares on his title page, is Cervantes's *Don Quixote*. Parson Adams is clearly an imitation of Cervantes's Knight of the Woeful Countenance. Both men share the same childlike innocence, unworldly absent-mindedness and comical appearance; both have the same tendency to blunder into battles and to take up the cause of innocence out of a spontaneous impulse, in defiance of prudence and commonsense. Where Don Quixote sees the world through a vision of chivalric romance, Adams sees it through the eyes of Aeschylus and the spirit of the New Testament. In narrative terms too the adventures, accidents and encounters of Adams, Joseph and Fanny on their travels through England imitate the various escapades of Don Quixote and Sancho Panza in Spain. A contemporary

3

reviewer of *Joseph Andrews* remarked that Fielding 'fails to consider the novel of *Don Quixote* as more than, generally speaking, a portrayal of Spanish customs', but this is far from true. On the contrary, Fielding effectively reproduces the two-fold character of the picaresque journey as it features in such works as *Don Quixote*. The routes of such journeys are designed to chart two simultaneous but separate kinds of progress. In external terms the picaresque journey offers a perfect vehicle for a series of satiric attacks on all the vices and affectations of society, as a whole gallery of characters, from noblemen to stable-boys and from chamber-maids to dowagers, pass before our eyes. But in addition the picaresque journey represents an interior quest for self-knowledge, as the youthful hero – in this case Joseph – gains in wisdom and maturity through combating the temptations that lie in the path of true felicity. In this way the journey of the *picaro* (Spanish for 'rogue') is a modernized, secular version of the journey of the ancient hero of classical epic, or the quest of the chivalric knight for the Holy Grail. In the Preface Fielding's narrator distinguishes his 'comic epic-poem in prose' from such true epics as the *Odyssey* or such true romances as *Cleopatra*, *Cassandra* or the *Grand Cyrus*. Yet the very fact that he mentions these affinities confirms that his own work is a changeling offspring from these traditional literary families.

In fact, one might argue that the narrator's Preface is less important for the things it says than for the manner in which it says them. The tongue-in-cheek boast that *Joseph Andrews* belongs to ' a species of writing which I have affirmed to be hitherto unattempted in our language' is a piece of comic provocation imitated from John Gay's preface to his 'tragi-comi-pastoral farce', *The What D'Ye Call It*. There Gay had declared: 'As I am the first who has introduced this kind of dramatic entertainment upon the stage, I think it absolutely necessary to say something by way of preface.'

Like Gay, Fielding wants to have it both ways and demonstrate that his work is both original and traditional. He wishes to prove its classical pedigree and formal correctness, while boasting of its freedom of invention and naturalness of style. This new young boisterous species is a changeling, a new combination of art and nature in which nature is given the upper hand, but which still requires the acknowledgement of the traditional authorities. In the same way it is only when those 'natural' children, Fanny and Joseph, are proved to be the legitimate offspring of respectable and well-established families that they achieve the final seal of approval on their lives of natural simplicity.

This duality between art and nature, authority and spontaneity, is fundamental to Fielding's work, and can be seen in many aspects of this novel. Thus, if one were to judge the 'moral' of the work purely in terms of what the characters say and do, one would accept that Fielding's aim was to endorse and recommend the childlike innocence and good-natured idealism of Parson Adams. Undoubtedly that is part – a very important part – of the novel's meaning. Yet one should not ignore another major element which contributes to the novel's total effect, that is, the narrator's tone. The narrator, unlike Adams, is urbane, sophisticated and knowing. His ironic tone and satiric insights reveal a consummate worldliness that Adams lacks. When the narrator conveys the increasing desperation of Slipslop's sexual frustration by remarking that she believed 'by so long self-denial she had ... laid up a quantity of merit to excuse any future failings' (I, 6), we recognize the confident wit of a connoisseur of human nature. The narrator has a perfect ear for euphemism and hypocrisy. He nicely catches the tone of indignant disbelief with which Lady Booby greets Joseph's defence of his virtue (I, 8). Again, when Betty the chambermaid, inflamed with desire for Joseph Andrews, finds relief for her pent-up frustration with Mr Tow-wouse, the narrator remarks that her 'passions were already raised, and which were not so whimsically capricious that one man only could lay them' (I, 18). This ironic use of the word 'capricious' here stands the normal meaning of the word on its head. In this instance fidelity (to Joseph) is represented as whimsical caprice, while promiscuity is treated as a form of consistency. This is a kind of ironic insight quite alien to Parson Adams, who does not even know the meaning of the word 'coquette'.

It is interesting to note that on several occasions the sentiments of Adams and those of the narrator coincide. When Adams rhapsodizes on the superior joys of mental, as opposed to physical, travel, this prepares the reader for the narrator's preference for the imaginative truth of literature over the factual truth of history in the following chapter (III, 1). Similarly the little lecture which Adams delivers on classical literature could easily pass for one of the narrator's digressions and, in fact, his remarks on Homer's 'lost' comedy, *Margites* (III, 2), exactly echo the narrator's words in the Preface. And, of course, the values which both endorse – good nature, Christian charity and benevolence – are identical. What is different is the tone in which these attitudes are expressed. Adams is open, ingenuous and spontaneous in all he says and does – unable to tell a lie, and instinctively inspired to dance at the sight of human happiness. The narrator, on the other hand, is oblique and subtle, convey-ing his true opinions ironically through exaggerated mock-eulogies for the hypocrisies and euphemisms that he exposes. Thus he assures us that he is 'sufficiently convinced' of the innocence of the constable who allowed a thief to escape, 'having been positively assured of it, by those who received their informations from his own mouth; which, in the opinion of some moderns, is the best and indeed only evidence' (I, 16). Part of Adams's charm comes from the fact that he instinctively always takes people at their word; the narrator's tone here, however, invites us to contemplate the discrepancy between public statement and private motive. It is the combination of these two tones, the ingenuous and the ingenious, that gives this novel its characteristic humour. For to express, as the narrator does, a love of unworldly innocence in a tone of urbane irony is itself richly ironic.

Already it will have been noticed that the term 'duality' has been used several times in describing Fielding's style. Such duality, antithesis or balance is not only characteristic of Fielding's literary technique, but is also typical of the literature of the period. No literary device is more common in Augustan poetry and prose than the antithesis, the formal balance and opposition of contrasting terms. Antithesis is the key not only to the style, but also to much of the morality of Pope's poetry. When, for example, in *Windsor Forest* (1713) he describes the landscape of Windsor in the following terms, he is doing far more than depicting a pretty scene:

> *Here hills and vales, the woodland and the plain,*
> *Here earth and water seem to strive again,*
> *Not Chaos-like together crush'd and bruis'd,*
> *But as the world, harmoniously confus'd:*
> *Where order in variety we see,*
> *And where, tho' all things differ, all agree.*

For Pope, the successful resolution of these warring antitheses through the revelation of a harmony behind the confusion and an order behind the variety represents a proof of divine Providence. Similarly the poet, playing God in the little world of his own artistic creation, arranges his descriptive terms in a pattern of antitheses, which indicates a central order and authority. Swift's satire in *Gulliver's Travels* exploits some central structural antitheses in the contrasts between the Lilliputians and the Brobdingnagians, or between the Houyhnhnms and the Yahoos. For the Augustans the formal representation of the world as a series of contrasting or complementary opposites provided a perfect model for an intellectual system of divide and rule. Such oppositions, which neatly evoke the familiar adversarial structure of debate, offered a basis for the rational analysis and categorization of even the most abstruse questions. In this way even doubts and uncertainties could be given a formal status in a coherent and regular system. Nor were such habits of mind and expression confined to those writers who saw themselves as custodians of a classical tradition. Even Defoe, who shared few of the neo-classical attitudes of Pope and Swift, developed his own system of moral antitheses using the language of profit and loss. When newly shipwrecked on the island, Crusoe draws up a balance sheet of his situation 'very impartially, like debtor and creditor'. Under the column for 'evil' or debit we find: 'I am cast upon a horrible desolate island, void of all hope of recovery.' Against this, in the 'good' or credit column, we read: 'But I am alive, and not drowned as all my ship's company was.' And so on. At the end of the statement Crusoe characteristically arrives at a conclusion which is equally satisfying in Christian or in capitalist terms, with a tidy profit 'on the credit side of the accompt'.

We have already noted Fielding's use of the antithesis in his distinction between burlesque and comedy. Further analysis of the Preface to *Joseph Andrews* reveals a consistent pattern of similar contrasts. The second paragraph begins: 'The epic as well as the drama is divided into tragedy and comedy.' This offers us two further contrasting pairs of terms: epic and drama, tragedy and comedy. Later in the Preface we encounter a sentence so symmetrically arranged that its key terms can almost be choreographed, like figures in a formal dance. One might represent the balancing phrases diagrammatically:

Now what *caricatura* is in painting,
          burlesque is in writing;
and in the same manner
          the comic writer
          and painter
                    correlate to each other.
And here I shall observe, that as
in the former, the painter seems to have the advantage;
                              so it is
in the latter infinitely on the side of the writer:
for the *monstrous* is much easier to paint than describe,
and the *ridiculous* to describe than paint.

Once again the symmetrical *form* in which such critical opinions are expressed is clearly as significant as the abstract meaning of the arguments themselves. Indeed, modern readers should not spend too long attempting to puzzle out the precise distinctions between burlesque and caricature, or between ridicule and comedy. It is more important to recognize the narrator's confident skill in arranging aesthetic and philosophical problems into these satisfying verbal patterns, thereby conveying a comforting illusion of truth. Following this confident demonstration of his ability to subdue the unruly chaos of art and literature into these neat antithetical categories, Fielding's narrator can proceed to lay down his own rules and divisions. 'The only source of the true ridiculous (as it appears to me) is affectation.' This simple assertion has the same magisterial tone as Pope's revelation in his poetic *Epistle to Cobham* that all the varieties of human folly can be traced back to a single source in the ruling passion:

> *Search then the Ruling Passion: There alone,*
> *The wild are constant and the cunning known;*
> *The fool consistent, and the false sincere;*
> *Priests, princes, women, no dissemblers here.*
> *This clue once found, unravels all the rest ...*

Both declarations have a confident theoretical clarity which proves less clear in practice. Readers will have a difficult task attempting to trace back all the various episodes in the book to this single source of affectation. Fielding's narrator acknowledges that strict adherence to this theoretical principle is impossible, and that he has occasionally strayed beyond the boundaries of affectation into the territories of vice. For, as he confesses, 'it is very difficult to pursue a series of human actions and keep clear from them' (the vices, that is). Having made this assertion of the 'only source of the true ridiculous', he quickly returns to his familiar technique of contrast and division, arguing that 'affectation proceeds from one of these two causes, vanity, or hypocrisy'. From this point he proceeds with a binary system of antitheses: art versus nature, head versus heart, vice versus virtue, good versus evil. It is through the deployment of such antithetical terms that the novel's morality works.

The Preface makes a number of interesting points, but readers should not be bamboozled into taking all Fielding's classical references and theoretical pronouncements at face value. The good-natured ridicule of affectation, we learn, is to be the central purpose of the book. However, the style reassures us that the innocence recommended is one strictly compatible with an urbane sense of humour and a worldly wit.

Before leaving this point, it may be worth noting how many of the incidental episodes in the novel resolve themselves into debates on moral and social issues. It may be a legal dispute between a surgeon and a parson, or a doctrinal debate between Adams and Barnabas on the theme of faith versus good works, but the antithetical structure is never far from the surface. In part this may reflect Fielding's familiarity with the forms of adversarial argument as a lawyer on the Western circuit. Certainly lawyers and legal questions figure prominently in these pages, and the narrator sometimes appears like a judge, summing up the evidence of the witnesses who appear before us.

In this respect one might note a further small point of similarity between Adams and the narrator. In the midst of his homily to Joseph to avoid despair after the abduction of Fanny, Adams remarks, 'I should indeed have said our ignorance is twofold (but I have not at present time to divide properly)' (III, 11). Division, as even Adams recognizes, is the fundamental process of categorization that allows human reason to control and explain the phenomena of nature and experience. The process of classification was very dear to the Augustan mind. Indeed, classification is at the very heart of classicism, with its ordered patterns based upon generic distinctions and hierarchical divisions. The narrator deliberately draws attention to his chapter divisions as a means of reinforcing his control over his fictional material, reminding us that what is presented is specifically formulated to satisfy our need for order:

> Then Joseph made a speech on charity, which the reader, if he is so disposed, may see in the next chapter; for we scorn to betray him into any such reading, without first giving him warning. (III, 5)

However, if the narrator's ostentatious technique of divide and rule in the Preface and first chapter of the novel represent an accurate introduction to the style and tone of much that follows, this cannot be said of the proliferation of literary allusions in these chapters. It is true that echoes of Homer and imitations of Cervantes mingle with Christian parables and contemporary disputes in the allusive pattern of the book. But the repeated jibes at Cibber with which the reader is assaulted in these opening chapters are not continued. And, as we shall see, the parody of Richardson's *Pamela* does not really extend beyond Chapter 10. Fielding evidently realized that his best method of challenging Richardson's style of writing was not through a tit-for-tat parody, but by offering us an alternative form of mimesis. *Joseph Andrews* is Fielding's first attempt at a novel which offers a morality of nature conveyed through the medium of art.

Characterization

Fielding begins the first chapter of *Joseph Andrews* with 'a trite but true observation: that examples work more forcibly on the mind than precepts'. Accordingly, we are not surprised to find a strong exemplary strain in many of his characters. He goes on to argue that 'by communicating such valuable patterns to the world, he [a writer] may perhaps do a more extensive service to mankind than the person whose life originally afforded the pattern'. Richardson too intended a strong exemplary element in his characterization. In the Preface to *Clarissa* he declares that his heroine 'is proposed as an exemplar to her sex' and that 'as far as is consistent with human frailty ... she is perfect'. Richardson wished his readers to be inspired by the unique piety and singular saintliness of his virtuous characters. His purpose, he stated, was 'above all to investigate the highest and most important doctrines not only of morality, but of Christianity, by showing them thrown into action in the conduct of the worthy characters; while the unworthy, who set those doctrines at defiance, are condignly, and, as may be said, consequentially, punished'.

Fielding's characters, however, are not unique but universal. 'I describe not men but manners', he writes in Book III, Chapter 1; 'not an individual, but a species.' He emphasizes this point by asserting that the lawyer he describes 'is not only alive, but hath been so these 4,000 years'. For Parson Adams too the physical world around him has no greater reality than the world of Aeschylus and the Bible. Indeed, his idea of 'modern times' is, as he confesses, 'these last thousand years' (II, 9). In a somewhat patrician manner Fielding despised the dramatic immediacy and highly detailed descriptions of *Pamela* as a combination of voyeurism and vulgarity. He preferred to adhere to neo-classical principles and deal with large, universal truths rather than with minute particularities.

Parson Adams, as we are explicitly informed in the Preface to *Joseph Andrews*, is intended as 'a character of perfect simplicity' whose 'goodness of heart will recommend him to the good-natur'd'. He is also an imitation – almost a reincarnation – of Don Quixote, with his comic blend of unworldly innocence and Christian idealism in the face of all adversity. Time and again we are clearly told of Adams's lack of worldly wisdom. In Chapter 3 we learn that he was 'as entirely ignorant of the ways of this world as an infant just entered into it could possibly be. As he had never any intention to deceive, so he never suspected such a design in others.'

Or again, Adams 'never saw further into people than they desired to let him' (I, 10).

Peter Pounce, we are informed, 'was a hypocrite, a sort of people whom Mr Adams never saw through' (III, 12). Yet this naïvety and gullibility, which frequently leads Adams into scrapes and misadventures, is viewed not as a weakness but as a strength. Adams's lack of worldliness, his simple idealism and imprudent impetuosity make him a model of Christian innocence. Travelling through the country with his beloved Aeschylus in one hand and his trusty crabstick in the other, he becomes a kind of pilgrim, on a journey whose episodes are shaped as much by classical myths and Christian models as by the accidents of landscape. Like Don Quixote his imagination transforms the physical landscape until it resembles the route of *The Odyssey* or *The Pilgrim's Progress* as much as a ramble through the inns and parishes of Wessex. As he remarks to the innkeeper who was once a sailor, all real travel is in the imagination:

'... Do you imagine sailing by different cities or countries is travelling? No.

Cælum non animum mutant qui trans mare currunt.

I can go farther in an afternoon, than you in a twelve-month. What, I suppose you have seen the Pillars of Hercules, and perhaps the Walls of Carthage. Nay, you may have heard Scylla, and seen Charybdis ... nay, you may have been on the banks of the Caspian, and called at Colchis, to see if there is another golden fleece.' – 'Not I truly master,' answered the host, 'I never touched at any of these places.' 'But I have been at all these,' replied Adams ... 'the travelling I mean is in books, the only way of travelling by which any knowledge is to be acquired ...' (II, 17)

This is just one of several occasions where Fielding allows Adams's unworldliness to appear both naïve and vain; his peremptory dismissal of all practical and worldly wisdom not only borders on an insensitive arrogance, but also involves him and his companions in a number of difficulties which could, with a little prudence and circumspection, have been avoided. For Adams is not without faults. Chief among these is a pedagogic vanity at his skills as a schoolmaster and preacher. He can, he believes, 'without much vanity' agree with Joseph when he calls him 'the best teacher of a school in all our country' (II, 5). He is likewise certain that his collection of manuscript sermons is 'as well worth a hundred pounds as a shilling was worth twelve pence' (I, 16). It is not that we necessarily disbelieve these claims, but they reveal an innocent naïvety concerning worldly values and an equally ingenuous display of pride. He also has a habit of becoming 'warm', that is irascible, on matters of principle, despite his frequent homilies on the necessity of curbing intemperate emotions. Thus in Book II, Chapter 11 Adams offers 'some

29

philosophical observations on the folly of growing warm in disputes', yet within a couple of sentences he becomes so vehement and violent in his dispute with the magistrate that, but for the intervention of Fanny, the two men would have come to blows. And throughout the book blows are frequently exchanged as Adams, displaying an enthusiastic brand of muscular Christianity, instinctively employs his crabstick and fists in defence of innocence in distress. Likewise in Book IV, Chapter 8 Adams counsels Joseph never to give way to immoderate grief, whatever the provocation, and to 'submit in all things to the will of Providence'. A few sentences later a messenger arrives to inform Adams that his youngest son has drowned, and Adams naturally 'began to stamp about the room and deplore the loss with the bitterest agony'. Volte-face effects of this kind are not designed to reveal character in any deep or psychological manner. Instead, they confirm the control of the narrator, trapping and exposing his characters in these situations of dramatic irony. The discrepancy between what Adams preaches and what he practises is revealed as a little comic vanity, or as a natural human vulnerability, but not as the conscious deception of an accomplished hypocrite.

Parson Adams, then, is designed as a universal type. In creating him, Fielding has endeavoured to give us the kind of timeless character that Samuel Johnson claimed could be found in the plays of Shakespeare: 'They are the genuine progeny of common humanity, such as the world will always supply, and observation will always find'. Yet there is nothing vague or indistinct about this portrait. Though unworldly, Adams is decidedly not ethereal. Fielding's aim in this character seems to be to combine a strong sense of physical enjoyment and human weakness with Christian idealism. Adams is no pious saint like Pamela, but a man with a robust, healthy and unashamed appetite for life's pleasures, for cakes and ale and song. He is an incongruous idealist, irascible, often pedantic, slightly pompous. We are constantly told of his childlike naïvety and unworldliness, though he stoutly defends his own knowledge of men and the world. His occasional failures to practise as he preaches reflect not hypocrisy but an impetuous tendency to get carried away by his feelings and to leap in without sufficient regard for practical consequences. One of the only two occasions on which he and Joseph disagree is just such a case. Adams cautions Joseph against having too great a fondness for carnal affections – even for the love of his wife-to-be, Fanny (IV, 8). This is a stoic counsel which is belied by his own conduct and, as his wife assures us, by his own love of family life.

Perhaps the most significant feature of Adams's character is the way he reacts physically and instinctively to all moral issues. Good and evil affect him as physical sensations of pleasure or pain, causing him to dance, or jump, or snap his fingers. When he is told of a bookseller who may be happy to publish his sermons, he 'snapt his fingers (as was usual with him) and took two or three turns about the room in an extasy' (I, 17). When a mean and surly innkeeper suggests the amputation of Joseph's injured leg, 'Adams fetched two strides across the room; and snapping his fingers over his head muttered aloud, "he would excommunicate such a wretch for a farthing: for he believed the devil had more humanity"' (II, 5). When, in the course of his lengthy tale, Mr Wilson relates how Providence seemed at last to have blessed him by giving him a lottery ticket worth £3,000, 'Adams snapt his fingers at these words in an ecstasy of joy' (III, 3). At another point in Wilson's narrative, when he confessed to having debauched a poor girl, 'Adams started up, fetched three strides cross the room, and then replaced himself in his chair' (III, 3). He capers, and more especially dances spontaneously at the sight or description of goodness. Should any prudish readers be offended by the lusciousness of the description of Joseph's encounter with Fanny (II, 12), the narrator advises them 'to take their eyes off from it, and survey Parson Adams dancing about the room in a rapture of joy'. When a poor pedlar offers to lend him six shillings and six-pence, 'Adams gave a caper' with pleasure (II, 15).

This is a completely natural and spontaneous kind of dancing; dancing for the joy of life. As such it has nothing at all in common with the superficial accomplishment in mechanical movements that was taught by contemporary dancing-masters. In one grotesque sequence Adams encounters one of these creatures, a lame German dancer (both of those terms, 'lame' and 'German', are deliberately chosen to indicate how alien his skills are from natural English movements). This dancing-master is among the group of practical jokers who aim to make Adams dance by pinning fire-crackers to his cassock. 'Adams being a stranger to this sport, and believing he had been blown up in reality, started from his chair, and jumped about the room, to the infinite joy of the beholders, who declared he was the best dancer in the universe' (III, 7). This mirthless mocking humour is as devoid of humanity as the cruel spectacle of enforced 'dancing' is devoid of the natural joy of dance.

Often it is Adams's comical and bedraggled appearance that leads him to be ridiculed and abused by those who judge the inner man by the outer clothes. He relates, without bitterness, how he had failed to gain a living promised to him by Sir Thomas Booby, because Lady Booby 'did not think my dress good enough for the gentry at her table' (II, 8). Parson Trulliber, seeing Adams's ragged clothes, and mistaking him for a pig-farmer, subsequently delivers a 'long oration on the dignity of the cloth' (II, 14). We are frequently reminded what a comical figure Adams is. When Slipslop first sees him, she mistakes him for 'a person travelling to a neighbouring fair with the thimble and button' (II, 3), that is, a tinker or fair-ground trickster. At various times he is covered with mud, drenched with hog's-blood; his cassock and gown are torn by briars and ripped to shreds by the hounds set to hunt him. In Book III, Chapter 12 we have this colourful description of his appearance:

... he had risen in such a violent hurry, that he had on neither breeches nor stockings; nor had he taken from his head a red spotted handkerchief, which by night bound his wig, that was turned inside out, around his head. He had on his torn cassock, and his great-coat; but as the remainder of his cassock hung down below his great-coat; so did a small strip of white, or rather whitish linnen appear below that; to which we may add the several colours which appeared on his face, where a long piss-burnt beard, served to retain the liquor of the stone pot, and that of a blacker hue which distilled from the mop.

The sight of such a figure is sufficient to 'disorder the composed gravity' of the facial muscles of even so humourless a person as Peter Pounce.

Adams has no use for outer show or fashionable activities. When Wilson describes to him in detail the lifestyle of a man of fashion who spends two hours dressing himself, two hours dining, and the rest of the day gossiping or spreading scandal in coffee-houses, playhouses and drawing-rooms, Adams is shocked and affronted. 'Sir, this is below the life of an animal,' he remarks vehemently, 'hardly above vegetation' (III, 3).

Yet, when it comes to matters of religion and the Church, Adams is a stickler for forms, a strict adherent to all the proper ceremonies and rituals. No amount of impetuous pleading by Joseph will persuade Adams to abridge the strict forms of Christian betrothal in favour of a wedding by special licence. When in church Adams demands respect as a representative of the Church, not as a mere man.

It was his maxim, that he was a servant of the Highest, and could not, without departing from his duty, give up the least article of his honour, or of his cause, to the greatest earthly potentate. Indeed he always asserted, that Mr Adams at church with his surplice on, and Mr Adams without that ornament, in any other place, were two very different persons. (IV, 16).

In the character of Adams the combination of Christian innocence with benign paternalism is triumphantly realized. The images of him with his pipe and ale, or blundering into battle with his crabstick, or displaying his schoolmasterly love of the classics, are all beautifully blended. When it comes to the character of Joseph Andrews, however, Fielding has more difficulties in achieving a convincing combination of sexual innocence with youthful vitality. The problem lies in the satiric origins of the book. For the first ten chapters of the novel the tone hovers uncertainly between burlesque and comedy. After that point, with Joseph's departure from London, the book begins to develop a picaresque form of its own. Until then it is essentially a parody of *Pamela*. In particular Joseph's two letters home to his sister (I, 6, 10) deliberately imitate the tone of wide-eyed innocence of Pamela's own epistolary style. Here is Joseph:

> O Pamela, my mistress is fallen in love with me – that is, what great folks call falling in love, she has a mind to ruin me; but I hope, I shall have more resolution and more grace than to part with my virtue to any lady upon earth. (I, 10)

Here, for a comparison, is a characteristic extract from one of Pamela's letters to her parents.

> O my dear mother, I am miserable! truly miserable! – But yet, don't be frighted, I am honest! And I hope God, of his goodness, will keep me so!
>
> O this angel of a master! this fine gentleman! this gracious benefactor to your poor Pamela! ... This very gentleman (yes, I *must* call him gentleman, though he has fallen from the merit of that title) has degraded himself to offer freedoms to his poor servant ... But be it as it will, all the use he can make of it will be, that he may be ashamed of *his* part; I not of *mine*: for he will see I was resolved to be virtuous, and gloried in the honesty of my poor parents. (Letter X)

Joseph's comic defence of his virtue in these chapters – the word 'virtue' is used twenty-five times in these first ten chapters – turns him into a figure of fun. He appears as an absurdly priggish innocent in scenes of ludicrous situation comedy. In her second attempt at seduction, Lady Booby, 'laying her hand carelessly upon his', presses him.

> 'What would you think, Joseph, if I admitted you to kiss me?' Joseph reply'd, 'he would sooner die than have any such thought.' 'And yet, Joseph,' returned she, 'ladies have admitted their footmen to such familiarities; and footmen, I confess to you, much less deserving them; fellows without half your charms: for such might almost excuse the crime. Tell me, therefore, Joseph, if I should admit you to such freedom, what would you think of me? – tell me freely.' 'Madam,' said Joseph, 'I should think your ladyship condescended a great deal below yourself.' 'Pugh!' said she, 'that I am to answer to myself: but would not you insist on more? Would you be contented with a kiss? Would not your inclinations be all on fire rather by such a favour?' 'Madam,' said Joseph, 'if they were, I hope I should be able to controll them, without suffering them to get the better of my virtue.' (I, 8)

The Priapus joke too (I, 2) seems designed to emphasize the comic shallowness of Joseph's character rather than to give him extra depth. His first job, we are told, was to act as a kind of scarecrow: 'His office was to perform the part the ancients assigned to the God Priapus, which deity the moderns call by the name of Jack-o'-Lent.' But Priapus was the Greek god of fertility, usually represented in statues as a grotesque dwarf with a huge phallus. It is of course ironic that Joseph, a model of chastity, should be called upon to fulfil such a role, but the irony seems to flatten him to a cartoon rather than filling him out to be a full character. Much the same might be said of the narrator's way of insisting on the significance of Joseph's name. On the seventh day after the death of Sir Thomas Booby, his widow 'ordered Joey, whom for good reason we shall hereafter call JOSEPH to bring up her tea-kettle' (I, 5). The 'good reason' hinted at is that Joey's behaviour with Lady Booby is similar in certain ways to the behaviour of Joseph towards Potiphar's wife (Genesis 39: 7–20), though the parallel is far from exact. Joey's position in the Booby household is far less exalted than Joseph's in the house of Potiphar; Sir Thomas Booby is dead, whereas Potiphar was alive; Potiphar's wife, when her advances were rejected, made a false claim of attempted rape against Joseph and her husband had him imprisoned. This deliberate labelling of Joseph is hardly the subtle re-creation of a literary imitation; rather, the poor fellow is merely a peg upon which various literary allusions can be hung in Fielding's games of parody and burlesque.

The most important positive aspect of Joseph's character, to set against these elements of comic stereotyping, is his affinity with nature. He is useless as a scarecrow since 'his voice being so extremely musical, that it rather allured the birds than terrified them'. He is similarly disqualified for his next employment as a whipper-in of dogs, 'the dogs preferring the melody of his chiding to all the alluring notes of the huntsmen, who soon became so incensed at it, that he desired Sir Thomas to provide otherwise for him'. Joseph is instinctively and completely in harmony with the natural world, and this natural ease is similarly evident in the main description of him:

Mr Joseph Andrews was now in the one and twentieth year of his age. He was of the highest degree of middle stature. His limbs were put together with great elegance and no less strength. His legs and thighs were formed in the exactest proportion. His shoulders were broad and brawny, but yet his arms hung so easily, that he had all the symptoms of strength without the least clumsiness. His hair was of a nut-brown colour, and was displayed in wanton ringlets down his back. His forehead was high, his eyes dark, and as full of sweetness as of fire. His nose a little inclined to the roman. His teeth white and even. His lips full, red, and soft. His beard was only rough on his chin and upper lip; but his cheeks, in which his blood glowed, were overspread with a thick down. His countenance had a tenderness joined with a sensibility inexpressible. Add to this the most perfect neatness in his dress, and an air, which to those who have not seen many noblemen, would give an idea of nobility. (I, 8)

The strongest impression conveyed by this description is of vitality and strength. Fielding needs to assure us that Joseph's virtue does not proceed from any impotence or effeminacy, and that he is full of normal, healthy, red-blooded instincts. Words like 'brawny' and 'wanton', and physical details like his eyes 'as full of sweetness as of fire', his lips 'full, red, and soft' and his cheeks 'in which his blood glowed', are full of a lusty sensuality. Combined with this strength, though, is a perfectly natural gracefulness of form: 'His limbs were put together with great elegance and no less strength.' This is not the studied formal elegance of the drawing-room and the dancing-master, but the harmony of nature itself. In addition to strength and elegance Joey's 'countenance had a tenderness joined with a sensibility inexpressible'; as a child of nature he is not without finer feelings. Finally, we are told that his combination of so many ideal qualities of mind and body 'would give an idea of nobility'. This may be taken with the small detail that 'his nose a little inclined to the roman', which might seem trivial were it not for the fact that Fanny's nose too was 'just inclining to the Roman' (II, 12). These 'noble' and 'roman' elements in their descriptions indicate that our hero and heroine are not merely Rousseau-esque children of nature, but are, in fact, true aristocrats whose natural nobility shows through their humble dress. 'To conclude all,' the narrator says at the end of the description of Fanny, 'she had a natural gentility, superior to the acquisition of art.' Thus the language in which both their natural beauty and their virtuous conduct is expressed gives the clearest hints of the discovery scene of the novel's dénouement. Just as Fielding needed to give his new species of writing the dignity of a classical pedigree, so his vision of natural harmony is only accomplished when the natural and the social hierarchies have been brought into alignment.

Let's look at the description of Fanny in full.

Fanny was now in the nineteenth year of her age; she was tall and delicately shaped; but not one of those slender young women, who seem rather intended to hang up in the hall of an anatomist, than for any other purpose. On the contrary, she was so plump, that she seemed bursting through her tight stays, especially in the part which confined her swelling breasts. Nor did her hips want the assistance of a hoop to extend them. The exact shape of her arms, denoted the form of those limbs which she concealed; and tho' they were a little redden'd by her labour, yet if her sleeve slipt above her elbow, or her handkerchief discovered any part of her neck, a whiteness appeared which the finest Italian paint would be unable to reach.

Her hair was of a chestnut brown, and nature had been extremely lavish to her of it, which she had cut, and on Sundays used to curl down her neck in the modern fashion. Her forehead was high, her eye-brows arched, and rather full than otherwise. Her eyes black and sparkling; her nose, just inclining to the Roman; her lips red and moist, and her under-lip, according to the opinion of the ladies, too pouting. Her teeth were white, but not exactly even. The small-pox had left one only mark on her chin, which was so large it might have been mistaken for a dimple, had not her left cheek produced one so near a neighbour to it, that the former served only for a foil to the latter. Her complexion was fair, a little injured by the sun, but overspread with such a bloom, that the finest ladies would have exchanged all their white for it: add to these, a countenance in which tho' she was extremely bashful, a sensibility appeared almost incredible; and a sweetness, whenever she smiled, beyond either imitation or description. To conclude all, she had a natural gentility, superior to the acquisition of art, and which surprized all who beheld her. (II, 12)

The emphasis we see is on plumpness and ripeness. Her arms are 'a little redden'd by her labour'; her complexion 'a little injured by the sun'. The term 'injured' here is, of course, ironic. In fact, her ruddy sun-tanned complexion and limbs prove her healthy, natural vitality, while the pure whiteness of those parts of her body not exposed to the sun, so delicate that 'the finest Italian paint would be unable to reach', proves that she is by no means coarse-grained or vulgar. In fact, she is the perfect balance of purity and ripeness, chastity and vitality. Her lips 'red and moist' and her 'swelling breasts' hint at the promise of sensuality, barely kept under the control of virtue and discretion, just as her ripe form seems almost 'bursting through her tight stays'. Nor is she completely without a trace of feminine fashion-consciousness, though it extends no further than her hair, 'which she had cut, and on Sundays used to curl down her neck in the modern fashion'. It is worth noting that in London Joseph too succumbs to just the same amount of fashionable temptation. His hair, we are told, 'was cut after the newest fashion, and became his chief care'. In Fanny's case this little innocent vanity is a tiny blemish added to make her seem less of a saintly prig. In the same way Fielding also gives her a slight physical blemish, but softens it till it almost becomes an adornment: 'The small-pox had left one only mark on her chin, which was so large it might have been mistaken for a dimple.' In fact, the effect of this portrait is to present her as an ideal country maiden, pure and innocent, yet beautiful and tender as ripe fruit. This imagery is continued in the final description of her as a bride in the last chapter, where her clothes are 'cherry-coloured' and 'the bloom of roses and lilies might a little illustrate her complexion, or their smell her sweetness'. 'Undressing to her,' remarks the narrator, 'was properly discovering, not putting off ornaments: for as all her charms were the gifts of nature, she could divest herself of none' (IV, 16).

The emphasis on the natural and physical beauty of both Fanny and Joseph points to an interesting element in Fielding's characterization throughout the novel. This is the identification of virtue with beauty and health, and of vice and affectation with ugliness and disease. Let us take Mrs Tow-wouse: 'Her person was short, thin and crooked ... Her lips were two bits of skin, which, whenever she spoke, she drew together in a purse' (I, 14). Contrast these 'two bits of skin' with Fanny's 'red and moist' lips and you have the difference between their two characters summed up in a single image. Moreover, there is an obvious pun in the word 'purse', which conveys not only the idea of pursed lips, but also of meanness, a miser's purse shut tight and retentive. Contrast Mrs Tow-wouse's 'loud and hoarse' voice with Joseph's, 'so extremely musical that it rather allured the birds than terrified them', and you have the same kind of instant characterization. Or take the description of Beau Didapper:

Mr Didapper, or Beau Didapper, was a young gentleman of about four foot five inches in height. He wore his own hair, tho' the scarcity of it might have given him sufficient excuse for a periwig. His face was thin and pale: the shape of his body and legs none of the best; for he had very narrow shoulders, and no calf; and his gait might more properly be called hopping than walking. (IV, 9)

Contrast the dwarfish Didapper with the portrait of Joseph, who is 'of the highest degree of middle stature'. Joseph's shoulders are 'broad and brawny' and his legs 'formed in the exactest proportion', while Didapper 'had very narrow shoulders, and no calf'. Joseph's hair is 'displayed in wanton ringlets down his back', while Didapper is almost bald. The name Didapper itself may hint at homosexuality, since in Cornelius Agrippa's *Three Books of Occult Philosophy* (I, 24) the didapper appears in a list of creatures which are 'equivocally generated'. Later details suggest Didapper is based on Lord Hervey, whom Pope attacks as Sporus, 'that mere white curd of Asses milk' in his *Epistle to Dr Arbuthnot* (1735). The cumulative effect of these hints is to convey a sense of effeminacy, perversity and superficiality which is quite at odds with the honest virility of Joseph.

Perhaps the most obvious illustration of this form of visual characterization is the description of Slipslop:

She was a maiden gentlewoman of about forty-five years of age, who having made a small slip in her youth had continued a good maid ever since. She was not at this time remarkably handsome; being very short, and rather too corpulent in body, and somewhat red, with the addition of pimples in the face. Her nose was likewise rather too large, and her eyes too little; nor did she resemble a cow so much in her breath, as in two brown globes which she carried before her; one of her legs was also a little shorter than the other, which occasioned her to limp as she walked. This fair creature had long cast the eyes of affection on Joseph ... (I, 6)

This comic visual caricature shows clearly the affinities between Fielding's style and Hogarth's, to which he often alludes. Though in the Preface the narrator protests that 'he who should call the ingenious Mr Hogarth a burlesque painter, would, in my opinion, do him very little honour', it is clear that he, like Hogarth, relishes the freedom to fill out his canvas with allusive grotesques. Slipslop is both a visual and a moral contrast with Mrs Tow-wouse. Slipslop is fat and ruddy, while Tow-wouse is thin and pinched. Slipslop is compared to a cow: a vital if somewhat unflattering comparison. Tow-wouse is compared to a purse: mean and dry. Slipslop has the marks of excess and grossness, Tow-wouse the signs of avarice and selfishness.

Some readers may find this apparent identification of goodness with beauty and of ugliness with evil as naïve, if not offensive. How seriously Fielding believes in the parallel is an interesting question. Clearly the identification works at a symbolic level. Joseph's physical beauty, like his affinity with nature, can be seen as merely a physical metaphor for his good nature; it is the physical expression of that moral harmony which animates his whole personality. By contrast the ugliness of Mrs Tow-wouse or Beau Didapper is a physical embodiment of their perversion of natural instincts of generosity and warmth. This technique can be seen as an extension of the conventions of romance, in which the virtuous damsel is always beautiful and the ogres and dwarves who threaten her are ugly and deformed. Thus Cinderella, like Fanny, is beautiful beneath her rags and despite her poverty, while the ugly sisters, for all their wealth and vanity, can never be other than grotesques.

Yet there are some occasions when Fielding seems to suggest that this identification of moral and physical beauty may be more than a mere literary convention. On one occasion Fanny conceives an instinctive distrust of an innkeeper's wife because 'she was one of the sourest-fac'd women she had ever beheld'. On this occasion, however, she appears to be wrong, for this sour-faced woman happily agrees to defer payment of their bill. However, 'lest Fanny's skill in physiognomy should be called into question' (II, 15), the narrator promptly informs us that she does so not from any motive of charity or benevolence, but because she mistakenly believes that Adams is related to Mr Trulliber, whose 'gravity, austerity, reserve and the guesses of his great wealth' made him a figure to be feared in the parish. In other words Fanny's physiognomical assumptions were indeed correct, and the sourness of the woman's face did indeed indicate a corresponding sourness of spirit. In this way a person's face and figure can be seen as a truer indication of their character than their words, for their physiques are the creation of nature, whereas their words can be manipulated by all the resources of human artifice and cunning.

'Nature generally imprints such a portraiture of the mind in the countenance, that a skilful physiognomist will rarely be deceived' declares Parson Adams confidently (II, 17). Yet, since we are so often and so explicitly informed that 'Parson Adamss never saw further into people than they desired to let him' (I, 10), we may reasonably enough take this as a further example of Adam's benign naïvety. However, in Fielding's 'Essay on Knowledge of Characters of Men', we find him saying much the same thing: 'The passions of Men do commonly imprint sufficient Marks on the Countenance' (Wesleyan Edition, vol. 1, p. 157). The reason why human nature remains a puzzle, Fielding asserts, is largely 'owing chiefly to want of Skill in the Observer, that Physiognomy is of so little Use and Credit in the World'. For example, people are too easily deceived by facial expressions, mistaking 'austerity, or gravity of countenance' for wisdom and the 'glavering' smile of false good humour for the true frankness of good nature.

In the Preface to *Joseph Andrews* Fielding's narrator says, 'Surely he hath a very ill-framed mind, who can look on ugliness, infirmity, or poverty, as ridiculous in themselves.' The words 'ill-framed' are interesting here, suggesting that only the deformed in mind will attack the deformed in body. It is only when 'ugliness aims at the applause of beauty, or lameness endeavours to display agility', that their affectations become a proper subject for ridicule. That is, Fielding's narrator argues, he does not attack ugliness as such, but only those moral deformities of affectation and vice which produce an effect of grotesque comic incongruity. Thus the squire who sets about 'roasting' Parson Adams is a kind of epitome of perversity, delighting only in incongruity and unnatural effects. 'What distinguished him chiefly was a strange delight which he took in everything which is ridiculous, odious and absurd in his own species; so that he never chose a companion without one or more of these ingredients' (III, 7). This prototype of the Marquis de Sade makes a fetish of unnaturalness. In theory these distinctions are perfectly just; in practice they seem to favour a policy of comic eugenics.

In all these matters it is necessary to distinguish between the natural beauty of the body and the superficial adornments of cosmetics or dress. As we have seen, Adams's appearance is frequently a subject for ridicule: he is mistaken for a tinker (II, 3); he is covered in hog's-blood (II, 5) or with the contents of a chamber-pot (III, 12). He is trampled in the mire of a pig-sty (II, 14) and his wig is torn by dogs (III, 6). But all these humiliations relate to his careless *dress*. There is nothing that suggests ugliness in his person. In fact, physical descriptions of Adams himself, as opposed to his dress, are rather limited, though what is emphasized is his strength: and, as we saw with Joseph Andrews, physical strength combined with moral idealism forms the essence of Fielding's brand of muscular Christianity.

The contrast between physique and fashion is a familiar element in Fielding's attacks on vanity and affectation. In the interpolated tale of Leonora, or the Unfortunate Jilt (II, 4), the relative terms of the descriptions of Leonora's two suitors, Horatius and Bellarmine, tell us all we need to know about their moral qualities. Horatius's 'face and person were such as the generality allowed handsome, but he had a dignity in his air very rarely to be seen. His temper was of the saturnine complexion, but without the least taint of moroseness.' Bellarmine, by contrast, is described in terms of his clothes, 'which attracted the eyes of the company; all the smarts, all the silk waistcoats with silver and gold edging, were eclipsed in an instant . . . he had on a cut-velvet coat of a cinnamon colour, lined with a pink satten, embroidered all over with gold; his waistcoat, which was cloth of silver, was embroidered with gold likewise' (II, 4).

All this gaudy finery is a clear indication to us that Bellarmine is not to be trusted. It is the beginning of Mr Wilson's 'rake's progress' when, at the age of seventeen, he forms the ambition of becoming a fine London gentleman: 'the first requisites of which, I apprehended, were to be supplied by a tailor, a periwig-maker, and some few more tradesmen who deal in furnishing the human body'. Beau Didapper and the lame German dancing-master cannot correct, though they may conceal, the deficiencies of their souls and bodies by their trivial preoccupations with matters of fashion and etiquette. Even on her wedding-day, as already noted, Fanny's clothes have a becoming simplicity and naturalness, for she 'could be prevailed on by Pamela to attire herself in nothing richer than a white dimity night-gown'(IV, 16). Fanny's beauty is a miracle of nature, not of art: 'Undressing to her was properly discovering, not putting off ornaments: for as all her charms were the gifts of nature, she could divest herself of none.'

What follows from this is an interesting use of nakedness throughout *Joseph Andrews* as a metaphor for moral instincts. We are first made aware of the ironic possibilities of nakedness in the 'Good Samaritan' episode (I, 12) after Joseph has been robbed, beaten and stripped of his clothes. The word 'naked' is repeated nine times in this single chapter.

The thieves 'stript him entirely naked, threw him into a ditch and departed'. Joseph's nakedness is a symbol of his bare humanity, his need and vulnerability. 'Ha! here's three on's are sophisticated. Thou art the thing itself; unaccommodated man is no more but such a poor, bare, forked animal as thou art,' cries Lear in the storm, as he comforts the naked poor Tom, the living representative of a world of poor, naked wretches (*King Lear*, III, iv). Poor, naked Joseph is the thing itself. His nakedness cries out for shelter, and is also the symbol of his innocence. The postillion who first sees him declares 'that there was a man sitting upright as naked as ever he was born'. The association with a new-born baby emphasizes both these ideas of innocence and vulnerability. Yet the passengers in the coach deliberately misconstrue his vulnerability as a threat, and his moral need as a social affront. 'O *J-sus*,' cry'd the lady, 'A naked man! Dear coachman, drive on and leave him.' The lady's comments are full of ironies, as she unconsciously uses Christian vocabulary to express an utterly unchristian lack of charity, insisting that 'she had rather stay in that place for all eternity, than ride with a naked man'. The old gentleman seizes on Joseph's nakedness as an excuse for some lewd puns, while for Mrs Tow-wouse his nakedness merely indicates that she will be unlikely to make any money out of him. In all these reactions, then, Fielding exploits nakedness as a symbol for simple humanity, and demonstrates each character's adherence to a piece of social punctilio to evade their responsibilities to common humanity.

Again, at the end of the novel, in a comic scene of bedroom farce which betrays the influence of the theatre (IV, 14), Fielding plays off the sexual and moral associations of nakedness. Awakened by sounds of struggle, the naked Parson Adams blunders first into Slipslop's room, and then into Fanny's, where he lies down to sleep beside her. Yet he remains in almost as perfect a state of innocence as his namesake before the Fall. His first instinct is always to assist those in distress; only long afterwards does he remember the social decencies, and then is comically embarrassed: 'and now first recollecting he was naked, he was no less confounded than Lady Booby herself, and immediately whipt under the bed-clothes'. In the same way, when discovered in bed with Fanny, he protests, 'As I am a Christian, I know not whether she is a man or a woman.' It is a fitting comic climax that Adams, whose innocence and humanity embody a naked, natural honesty with no mask or cover, should be caught in this compromising situation. One might contrast his nakedness in this chapter with that of the grotesque Beau Didapper who 'disencumbered himself from the little clothes he had on' in order to enjoy the embraces of Slipslop, whom he mistakes for Fanny.

When in *Tom Jones* the philosopher Square is discovered 'among other female utensils' in Molly Seagrim's bedroom (*Tom Jones*, V, 5), the revelation deals an abrupt and decisive blow to his protestations of stoicism. By contrast the image of Adams in Fanny's bed only confirms the triumph of nakedness as moral virtue over nakedness as sexual threat.

It is noticeable that Bellarmine, the lame German dancing-master and Beau Didapper share more than the same taste for gaudy, ostentatious clothes; in addition they also favour an absurdly affected manner of speech, despising simple English and preferring a grotesque cosmopolitan argot. This too, in Fielding's eyes, is a sign of moral decay. Good plain English, like roast beef and English ale, is a symbol of intrinsic virtue, just as surely as foreign foods and fashions are symbols of affectation and vice. Later I shall deal in detail with his linguistic satire, but a few words on the subject of food might be appropriate here.

The fact that Fanny, Joseph and Adams all have good healthy appetites is a sure sign of their robust vitality. 'Hunger is better than a French cook,' remarks the narrator aphoristically (III, 8), and Fielding's virtuous trio are frequently hungry. We are repeatedly told that they 'enjoyed their homely but hearty meal' (IV, 12); or that they were entertained 'in the most splendid manner, after the custom of the old English hospitality which still is preserved in some very few families in the remote parts of England' (IV, 16); or that they 'fell to eating with appetites infinitely more voracious than are to be found at the most exquisite eating-house in the parish of St James's' (II, 16). What they eat is as important as their natural appetite. After his 'roasting' at the squire's house, Adams declares that he took 'much greater satisfaction' in his 'homely commons' of bread and cheese than in his splendid dinner. When Joseph expresses a desire for 'a piece of boiled beef and cabbage', it is a sign he is recovering from his beating (I, 15), and Fielding clearly endorses Adams's view that some good wholesome food will do more for the invalid than all the doctor's draughts and specifics (I, 15). Breakfast at the Adams's house, we learn, consists of a nourishing but homely dish of bacon and cabbage (IV, 8).

At the various inns which he encounters on his travels, Adams never fails to quench his thirst and smoke his pipe. Significantly it is nearly always beer or ale – and just very occasionally wine – that he drinks. He never touches spirits. Fielding, like his friend Hogarth, drew a clear distinction between the beneficial effects of good English ale and the pernicious consequences of gin. Hogarth's moralistic diptych, *Beer Street* and *Gin Lane* (1751), depicts the contrast. In *Beer Street* churches are being built, industry thrives, people are plump, affectionate and benign. In *Gin Lane* houses are crashing down and only the pawn-broker has a flourishing trade. Cadaverous figures gnaw at bones, bodies lie unburied and in the foreground a gin-sodden mother drops her baby to the ground in a parody of a madonna and child.

Fielding not only compares his own work with Hogarth's art in the Preface to *Joseph Andrews*, but there is also a direct and unmistakable analogy between the structure of *The Rake's Progress* and Mr Wilson's account of his own misadventures in London. It is a telling detail that among the many malicious pranks the 'roasting' squire causes to have inflicted upon Adams, he should 'convey a quantity of gin into Mr Adams's ale'. This single spiteful act is a perfect microcosm of the depraved tastes that the squire and his guests represent. Though homely, simple fare is constantly recommended, this should not be misconstrued as frugality, thrift or meanness. While food should not be ostentatious or Frenchified in the manner of the so-called 'new cookery', it should always be plentiful. The ripe plumpness which Fielding admires in Fanny goes with a lively appetite for the pleasures of the table. Just as chastity should not be mistaken for frigidity, so a plain, honest taste should not be mistaken for asceticism. Fielding stresses the enjoyment of nature's bounteous gifts. And when Peter Pounce remarks to Adams, 'How can any man complain of hunger ... in a country where such excellent sallads are to be gathered in almost every field?' (III, 13), this should not be taken as some excellent recommendation of a vegetarian high-fibre diet or an attack upon gross self-indulgence, but as an example of miserly greed and a lack of charity. Somewhere between the extremes of self-indulgence and miserly frugality is the middle path of natural, healthy enjoyment – which Fielding recommends. At the idyllic conclusion of Mr Wilson's tale, a 'rake's progress' miraculously saved from disaster at the last moment by Providence in the shape of a benign heiress, we have an image of that ideal middle path.

... vanity had no votary in this little spot, here was variety of fruit, and every thing useful for the kitchin, which was abundantly sufficient to catch the admiration of Adams, who told the gentleman he had certainly a good gardener. Sir, answered he, that gardener is now before you; whatever you see here, is the work solely of my own hands. Whilst I am providing necessaries for my table, I likewise procure myself an appetite for them. In fair seasons I seldom pass less than six hours of the twenty-four in this place, where I am not idle, and by these means I have been able to preserve my health ever since my arrival here without assistance from physick. Hither I generally repair at the dawn, and exercise myself whilst my wife dresses her children, and prepares our breakfast, after which we are seldom asunder during the residue of the day; for when the weather will not permit them to accompany me here, I am usually within with them; for I am neither ashamed of conversing with my wife, nor of playing with my children ...

... my Harriet I assure you is a notable housewife, and the house-keepers of few gentlemen understand cookery or confectionary better; but these are arts which she hath no great occasion for now: however, the wine you commended so much last night at supper, was of her own making as is indeed all the liquor in my house, except my beer, which falls to my province ... We formerly kept a maid-servant, but since my girls have been growing up, she is unwilling to indulge them in idleness; for as the fortunes I shall give them will be very small, we intend not to breed them above the rank they are likely to fill hereafter, nor to teach them to despise or ruin a plain husband. Indeed I could wish a man of my own temper, and a retired life, might fall to their lot: for I have experienced that calm serene happiness which is seated in content is inconsistent with the hurry and bustle of the world. (III, 4)

This idyllic scene concludes with Adams declaring 'that this was the manner in which people had lived in the golden age'. Such pictures of the life of retirement as an image of the golden age occur in several works of Augustan literature. Similar descriptions can be found in many of Pope's poems, and a close parallel appears in an underrated poem published just four years before *Joseph Andrews*, Matthew Green's *The Spleen*. Here too we find the same idealistic treatment of simple domesticity, and a bucolic scene bathed in a golden Horatian glow. This is Green's ideal spot:

> *A farm some twenty miles from town,*
> *Small, tight, salubrious, and my own;*
> *Two maids, that never saw the town,*
> *A serving-man not quite a clown ...*
> *One genial room to treat a friend,*
> *Where decent cupboard, little plate,*
> *Display benevolence, not state.*
> *And may my humble dwelling stand*
> *Upon some chosen spot of land:*
> *A pond before full to the brim,*
> *Where cows may cool, and geese may swim;*
> *Behind, a green like velvet neat,*
> *Soft to the eye, and to the feet;*
> *Where odorous plants in evening fair*
> *Breathe all around ambrosial air; ...*
> *There see the clover, pea, and bean,*
> *Vie in variety of green;*
> *Fresh pastures speckled o'er with sheep,*
> *Brown fields their fallow sabbaths keep ...*
> *Thus sheltered, free from care and strife,*
> *May I enjoy a calm through life.*

It is just such an ideal life that Joseph and Fanny embark upon at the end of *Joseph Andrews*. Joseph lays out the fortune of £2,000, given by Mr Booby to Fanny 'in a little estate in the same parish with his father, which he now occupies (his father having stock'd it for him) and Fanny presides, with most excellent management in his dairy; where, however, she is not at present very able to bustle much, being, as Mr Wilson informs me in his last letter, extremely big with her first child' (IV, 16). The strong sense of fecundity here is the final seal of natural approval on their lives. Throughout the novel family life, represented by Mr Wilson, Adams and finally Fanny and Joseph, is viewed as the ideal natural state which brings true happiness, free from the affectations and vanities of court and city life.

It is noticeable that most of the hypocritical characters are childless, a further indication of their self-centredness. Another interesting ingredient in the imaginative texture of the novel is supplied by Fielding's use of animal imagery. This not only allows him to draw a series of colourful and comic contrasts; it also helps to give a sense of physical force to what might otherwise be rather stereotyped and static sketches. Indeed, there are so many animal comparisons scattered throughout the book that the whole atmosphere has more of the farmyard than the drawing-room. One of the first and most striking of these concerns Slipslop. She, we have already been informed, does not 'resemble a cow so much in her breath, as in two brown globes which she carried before her' (I, 6). Now, however, she is compared to a much more predatory creature:

As when a hungry tygress, who long had traversed the woods in fruitless search, sees within the reach of her claws a lamb, she prepares to leap on her prey; or as a voracious pike, of immense size, surveys through the liquid element a roach or gudgeon which cannot escape her jaws, opens them wide to swallow the little fish: so did Mrs Slipslop prepare to lay her violent amorous hands on the poor Joseph ... (I, 6)

Obviously there's a tone of mock-heroic ridicule about this description, and the comedy really lies in the comparison of this plump, cowlike creature with anything as sleek, agile or dangerous as a tigress or pike. From this point onwards Slipslop's desires are symbolized as the vain dreams of a ruminant cow to become a rapacious tigress. It is the same hopeless ambition, or dream of greatness, which later prompts her to cast 'a look at Fanny not unlike that which Cleopatra gives Octavia in the play' (II, 13). This confirms both the mock-heroic comedy of her passion and the violence that desires can unleash. Nor should we forget that when Beau Didapper mistakenly gropes his way into her bed (IV, 14), she hugs him with some physical 'ardour' and, we are told, 'caught fast hold' of him. The predatory descriptions of Slipslop's passions may be directly contrasted with those of Fanný. Her embraces are described thus:

> Tho' her modesty would only suffer her to admit his eager kisses, her violent love made her more than passive in his embraces; and she often pulled him to her breast with a soft pressure, which, tho' perhaps it would not have squeezed an insect to death, caused more emotion in the heart of Joseph, than the closest Cornish hug could have done. (I, 11)

The pressure exerted here we see is both violent and delicate, emotional as well as physical, tender not destructive. It represents a perfect combination of natural warmth of feeling and instinctive modesty.

Parson Adams is compared to a whole menagerie of animals. His fist resembles the knuckle of an ox (I, 15); he is as brisk as a bee (III, 2); hunted like a jack-hare (III, 6); baited like a badger (III, 6); snores like a donkey (III, 6); runs as fast as a greyhound (II, 7); but is 'no chicken' (II, 9). All these animal similes give an additional physicality to the novel. The fact that Fielding instinctively draws his images and analogies from the farmyard rather than the country house contributes importantly to the tone and atmosphere of the work. Of course these are not the only familiar images that we encounter in this novel. Fielding also makes considerable use of the law courts and the theatre for key metaphors, and I shall examine the significance of these usages later. But this instinctive and pervasive recourse to animal imagery is one important element which helps to open out the atmosphere of the novel, and draw it away from being an enclosed literary satire.

However, animals in *Joseph Andrews* are not only used as metaphors. They are also physically present in considerable numbers, particularly dogs, hogs, birds and sheep. Often the situation or behaviour of these animals is used to offer a warning or prefiguration of what may befall the human characters since, as we have seen, Joseph in particular has a natural affinity with animals. At one point Adams, in the darkness of night, having just rescued Fanny, but without knowing it to be her, is surrounded by a group of young fellows 'who came to these bushes in pursuit of a diversion which they call *bird-batting*' (II, 10). This diversion, the narrator explains for the benefit of metropolitan readers, 'is performed by holding a large clap-net before a lanthorn, and at the same time, beating the bushes: for the birds, when they are disturbed from their place of rest, or roost, immediately make to the light, and so are enticed within the net' (II, 10). But very soon it is Fanny and Adams themselves who are trapped and netted. Holding the lanthorn to the parson's face, the huntsmen agree '*he had the most villainous countenance* they ever beheld'. Thus they give up their intention of hunting birds in favour of hunting humans, an activity 'promising them better sport'.

Fanny in particular is often seen as a timorous prey or quarry; sometimes as a bird, to be hunted and caged, sometimes as a lamb to be slaughtered. When she is abducted, the captain who seizes her shows no more consideration for her cries 'than a butcher hath of those of a lamb' (III, 9).

An interesting parallel with this use of animal imagery to prefigure or dramatize human misfortunes can be found in *Tom Jones*. There, the little episode concerning Sophia's pet bird (IV, 3) offers a vivid insight into the motives and characters of three of the novel's central figures. Tom, who like Joseph has an affinity with nature, had nursed the bird, taught it to sing and given it to Sophia when they were still in their early teens. She was extremely fond of the bird, which she called little Tommy, allowing it to 'perch upon her finger and lie contented in her bosom'. This tenderness naturally suggests to us a similar fondness for the bird's human namesake. But Blifil, jealous of her feelings for both Tom and Tommy, releases the bird, protesting that it seemed to him 'against the law of nature' to keep it tied by a string, for 'everything hath a right to liberty'. This device of claiming a noble motive for a mean action is typical of Blifil's character throughout the novel. Fielding rounds off this little scene with a characteristic irony, informing us in an aside that the bird was no sooner released than 'a nasty hawk carried it away'. Liberty brings its own dangers. A benign and tender protection is revealed as the best compromise between the constraints of society and the brutality of untamed nature.

At the beginning of Book III Joseph, Fanny and Adams are again travelling by night when they are terrified to overhear the voices of murderers, one of whom boasts of having 'killed a dozen since that day fortnight' (III, 2). Later they discover that these 'murderers' are in fact sheep-stealers, and once again the little band becomes a kind of substitute animal prey. Even in the midst of the pastoral idyll of Wilson's homestead, a sudden change of tone signals the ever-present threat of evil on the borders of this little Eden:

These good people were in the utmost cheerfulness, when they heard the report of a gun, and immediately afterwards a little dog, the favourite of the eldest daughter, came limping in all bloody, and laid himself at his mistress's feet. The poor girl, who was about eleven years old, burst into tears at the sight, and presently one of the neighbours came in and informed them, that the young squire, the son of the lord of the manor, had shot him as he past by, swearing at the same time he would prosecute the master of him for keeping a spaniel ... (III, 4)

The sudden jolt of this incident is a warning against complacency, and a reminder that even here, in this little image of the golden age, the threat of evil still lurks. This malicious slaughter of an innocent is completely motiveless, and the young squire, we are told, 'could have no motive but ill-nature'.

Yet it would be wrong to suggest that Fielding necessarily presents the killing of animals as a symbol of evil. Just a few pages later another animal is killed, this time a hare, and although Fanny's tender heart is sorely affected to see the suffering of this poor, defenceless creature, Joseph insists that there is no cause for distress since the hare 'was killed fairly' according to 'the laws of hunting'. The passage contains many interesting points and is worth quoting in full.

Whilst they amused themselves in this harmless and delightful manner, they heard a pack of hounds approaching in full cry towards them, and presently afterwards saw a hare pop forth from the wood, and crossing the water, land within a few yards of them in the meadows. The hare was no sooner on shore, than it seated itself on its hinder legs, and listened to the sound of the pursuers. Fanny was wonderfully pleased with the little wretch, and eagerly longed to have it in her arms, that she might preserve it from the dangers which seemed to threaten it: but the rational part of the creation do not always aptly distinguish their friends from their foes; what wonder then if this silly creature, the moment it beheld her, fled from the friend who would have protected it, and traversing the meadows again, past the little rivulet on the opposite side. It was however so spent and weak, that it fell down twice or thrice in its way. This affected the tender heart of Fanny, who exclaimed with tears in her eyes against the barbarity of worrying a poor innocent defenceless animal out of its life, and putting it to the extremest torture for diversion. She had not much time to make reflections of this kind, for on a sudden the hounds rushed through the wood, which resounded with their throats, and the throats of their retinue, who attended on them on horseback. The dogs now past the rivulet, and pursued the footsteps of the hare; five horsemen attempted to leap over, three of whom succeeded, and two were in the attempt thrown from their saddles into the water; their companions and their own horses too proceeded after their sport, and left their friends and riders to invoke the assistance of fortune, or employ the more active means of strength and agility for their deliverance. Joseph however was not so unconcerned on this occasion; he left Fanny for a moment to herself, and ran to the gentlemen, who were immediately on their legs, shaking their ears, and easily with the help of his hand attained the bank, (for the rivulet was not at all deep) and without staying to thank their kind assister, ran dripping across the meadow, calling to their brother sportsmen to stop their horses: but they heard them not.

The hounds were now very little behind their poor reeling staggering prey, which fainting almost at every step, crawled through the wood, and had almost got round to the place where Fanny stood, when it was overtaken by its enemies; and being driven out of the covert was caught, and instantly tore to pieces before Fanny's face, who was unable to assist it with any aid more powerful than pity; nor could she prevail on Joseph, who had been himself a sportsman in his youth, to attempt anything contrary to the laws of hunting, in favour of the hare, which he said was killed fairly. (III, 6)

The violence and cruelty of this scene are undisguised. Words like 'barbarity' and 'torture', together with the description of the hare being 'tore to pieces before Fanny's face' and later 'devoured', indicate the full brutality of this 'sport' or diversion. The instinctive tender sympathy of Fanny's reaction to this scene of wanton cruelty, together with the narrator's explicit comparison between human – 'the rational part of the creation' – and animal victims, leads us to expect an identification of interest between the innocent hare and our good-natured humans. Joseph's reaction, insisting that the hare 'was killed fairly', therefore comes as something of a surprise. The full description that we have of the hounds 'worrying a poor innocent defenceless animal out of its life' before tearing it to pieces informs us precisely what is meant by the word 'fairly' here. Moreover, it is somewhat surprising to find Joseph appealing to something called the 'laws of hunting', which sound suspiciously similar to those specious 'laws of honour' which Fielding attacks throughout his writings. Such 'laws' or codes customarily make a fetish of certain rituals or ceremonies in order to evade or pervert the clear and straightforward demands of conscience and morality. Even the word 'sportsman' here carries an unusual connotation, since almost every other time that the words 'sport' or 'sportsmen' occur in the book they operate as euphemisms for a kind of sadism. Tearing a hare to pieces is sport (III, 6); the 'roasting' squire is a great sportsman, who declares that 'parson-hunting was the best sport in the world' (III, 6); the gang of bird-batters also concludes that hunting humans is 'better sport' than netting birds (II, 10).

Fielding nicely contrasts Joseph's assistance to the hunters with Fanny's inability to assist the hunted. Joseph is inspired by a quasi-chivalric instinct to assist a fellow 'sportsman' for which, in fact, he is not even thanked. Fanny, on the other hand, 'was unable to assist [the hare] with any aid more powerful than pity'. The clear contrast between the ingratitude of the hunters and the innocence of the hare directs our sympathies towards Fanny's view of the scene. However, Fielding's purpose in having Joseph defend the 'laws of hunting', despite Fanny's tender-hearted protests, seems to be an attempt to emphasize his masculinity. Although chaste, Joseph is no milk-sop, and enjoys the normal lusty outdoor activities such as hunting just like any other red-blooded youth. While he would never condone cruelty, Joseph is prepared to accept 'sport' so long as it is 'fair'. In a sense too Fielding seems to imply that the cruelties of nature, including human nature, cannot be simply wished away with a tear; and that the sensible thing is to restrain them by rules, rather than attempt the impossible, that is, to purge them away completely. Hunting is also often a metaphor for sex, and this is almost a vicarious means for crediting Joseph with the lusty appetite of Tom Jones without violating his strict chastity. His only disagreements with Adams occur, as we have seen, when he rejects the parson's counsels of unnatural stoicism to protest his passionate nature. It is 'normal' for a man to hunt, hence Joseph hunts; in the same way, it is 'normal' for a girl to shrink from violence, and Fanny does so. Fielding's narrator describes the patterns of traditional nurture which produce these antithetical reactions with a tone of ironic mockery which stops short of implying any alternative.

> ... at the age of seven or something earlier, miss is instructed by her mother, that master is a very monstrous kind of animal, who will, if she suffers him to come too near her, infallibly eat her up, and grind her to pieces. That so far from kissing or toying with him of her own accord, she must not admit him to kiss or toy with her ... These impressions being first received, are farther and deeper inculcated by their school-mistresses and companions; so that by the age of ten they have contracted such a dread and abhorrence of the above named monster, that whenever they see him, they fly from him as the innocent hare doth from the greyhound. (IV, 7)

Hence in their reactions to the hunting scene, Joseph and Fanny may be seen enacting their prescribed gender roles. And while Fielding in this novel suggests that 'virtue' – that is, chastity – should not be seen as merely a female quality, he still draws a conventional distinction between masculine strength and feminine meekness. So, while there are several parallels between hunting animals and ensnaring humans throughout the novel, the same moral attitudes do not apply universally. Pope was almost alone in the eighteenth century in his condemnation of hunting. In the *Guardian* for 1713 he wrote:

> We should find it hard to vindicate the destroying of anything that has life, merely out of wantonness; yet in this principle our children are bred up, and one of the first pleasures we allow them, is the licence of inflicting pain upon poor animals: Almost as soon as we are sensible what life is ourselves, we make it our sport to take it from other creatures. (*Guardian*, no. 61, 21 May 1713)

For Fielding, however, hunting is part of the natural order. It is natural for hounds to hunt hares and for hawks to prey on smaller birds. What is not natural or acceptable is for huntsmen, with their blood up, to turn from pursuing a hare to unleashing their dogs on a poor parson.

The Violence of Virtue

One obvious way of gauging a writer's preoccupations, particularly those of a satirical writer like Fielding, is to examine the frequency with which certain key words and concepts occur in his works. *Joseph Andrews* is a novel dedicated to qualities of innocence, simplicity and good nature, and designed to ridicule vanity and affectation. Naturally, therefore, all of these words are sprinkled liberally throughout the text. Mr Wilson's narrative, a 'rake's progress' in miniature, demonstrates the dangers of vanity; and its concentration on this theme is underlined by the fact that the word 'vanity' occurs in it no less than nine times. 'Virtue' is another favourite word, particularly in the first ten chapters of the novel, where Fielding's parody of Richardson's *Pamela* is most evident. 'Charity' is another key term, repeated many times as different characters debate the complex social implications of this disconcertingly simple moral term. Yet in a work as simple, innocent and good natured as this, there is one word whose frequency comes as something of a shock. That is the word 'violence'. No one would think of *Joseph Andrews* as a violent book, though a casual glance through the main events of the plot would reveal a dozen or so fist-fights and cudgel-bouts, as well as hunts, ambushes and 'warm' disputes. The fact that so much violence does not actually strike us as dangerous or threatening is a result of the comic tone in which the narrator describes these episodes. By contrast the intense first-person drama of Pamela's narrative can evoke an atmosphere of violence and threat without any of the physical conflict of Fielding's novel. Consider the undertone of menace in this dialogue between Mrs Jewkes and Pamela:

> She came to me, and took me in her huge arms, as if I were a feather; said she, 'I do this to shew you, what a poor resistance you can make against me, if I pleased to exert myself; and so, lambkin,' setting me down, 'don't say to your *wolf*, "I *won't* come to bed!" But undress, undress I tell you. And, Nan, pray pull off my young lady's shoes.' 'No, pray don't,' said I, 'I will come to bed presently, since I can't help it.' (*Pamela*, 'Almost Twelve o'Clock, Saturday Night)

From the start Pamela's narrative is full of fear and apprehensions of violation. Her very first words are 'I have great trouble...' and throughout her story the most innocent domestic details are made to convey a sense of claustrophobia and threat. Contrasted with this, the brawls and bloodshed of *Joseph Andrews* appear almost festive:

Adams dealt him so sound a compliment over his face with his fist, that the blood immediately gushed out of his nose in a stream. The host being unwilling to be outdone in courtesy, especially by a person of Adams's figure, returned the favour with so much gratitude, that the parson's nostrils likewise began to look a little redder than usual. Upon which he again assailed his antagonist, and with another stroke laid him sprawling on the floor. (II, 5)

The mock-politeness of the language here turns the fight into a little pantomime, a comic exchange of physical formalities with no sense of pain or suffering. More usually Fielding combines mock-Homeric exaggeration with slapstick farce to obtain the same effect of burlesque ritual. The violence is transformed into a comic sequence, like a Laurel and Hardy film or a Tom and Jerry cartoon:

Hitherto Fortune seemed to incline the victory on the travellers side, when, according to her custom, she began to shew the fickleness of her disposition: for now the host entering the field, or rather chamber, of battle, flew directly at Joseph, and darting his head into his stomach (for he was a stout fellow, and an expert boxer) almost staggered him; but Joseph stepping one leg back, did with his left hand so chuck him under the chin that he reeled. The youth was pursuing his blow with his right hand, when he received from one of the servants such a stroke with a cudgel on his temples, that it instantly deprived him of sense, and he measured his length on the ground. (III, 9)

Often the comic exaggeration of the language actually has the effect of diminishing its impact. Blood 'gushes' or 'spurts'; people are 'drubbed' or 'thrashed'; they do not simply rise or walk but 'leap' and 'start'. This is the *splat! pow!* language of cartoon which allows the characters to bounce back in the next scene or chapter without a scratch on them. To that extent the violence of the vocabulary and action has the effect of diminishing the humanity and rationality of the characters, reducing them to comic automata. A great deal of the action – and particularly of the *re*actions – takes place at the double, like a piece of speeded-up film, and the result is not only comic in itself but actually leads to a number of accidents and collisions producing further comedy.

Let us look now at how the words 'violent' and 'violence' themselves are used. After Sir Thomas's death, Lady Booby confines herself to the house 'as closely as if she herself had been attacked by some violent disease' (I, 5). She attributes Joseph's inhibitions with her to his 'violent respect' for her (I, 5). Mrs Slipslop plans to lay 'violent amorous hands' on Joseph (I, 6). She is well acquainted with the 'violence of her lady's temper' (I, 7). The narrator defers to the 'violent modesty' of his female readers (I, 8). Lady Booby's 'violent passion' causes her to ring the bell 'with infinitely more violence than was necessary' (I, 8). Fanny's 'violent love' makes her more than passive in Joseph's embraces (I, 11). Betty the chambermaid lays 'violent hands' on the piece of gold stolen from Joseph (I, 14). Later Betty suffers 'violent agitation' at her disappointed hopes of intimacy with Joseph (I, 18). Horatius has a 'violent passion' for Leonora (II, 4), and Fanny, we are told, loves Joseph 'with inexpressible violence, though with the purest and most delicate passion' (II, 10). Adams is 'violent and positive' in his opinions (II, 11). Wilson's passions make a 'violent progress' (III, 3). The squire enjoys a 'violent fit of laughter' at the hunting of Adams (III, 7). Fanny is abducted 'by violence' (III, 9). Even grief (III, 11) and awe (IV, 1) are described as violent. People engage in violent litigation (IV, 10) or feel violent fury (IV, 10). There are several violent storms.

This list is far from exhaustive and readers will no doubt find many further examples of their own. What is the effect of all this violence? Firstly, I think, it reinforces the sense of sudden, hectic, thoughtless activities and reactions. We are dealing, in fact, with two separate but related meanings of the word 'violent'. The first is a simple intensifier, meaning strong or powerful, as in a violent colour or violent headache. The second relates to physical force and intimidation, as in a violent attack or assault. The curiously comic effect of all these violent feelings in *Joseph Andrews* comes from Fielding's merging of these two senses of the word. Violence, as he presents it, is an instinctive force, corresponding to natural feelings and spontaneous reactions. Violence has a direct line to the ruling passions, and in this way may be seen as the antithesis to affectation, and the antidote to hypocrisy. Hypocrisy, after all, depends on cunning and deliberate deception, whereas these violent rages and passions represent a character's true instincts. Thus Lady Booby's true feelings are revealed by the violent agitation of her moods. 'The lady had scarce taken two turns before she fell to knocking and ringing with great violence' (I, 7). In the nearest thing to a soliloquy that she can achieve, she asks grandly, 'Whither doth this violent passion hurry us?' (I, 8). So, if violence is demonstrated by the callous Trulliber and the 'roasting' squire, it is also shown by the impetuous Adams and the instinctive Joseph. In fact, as we have already seen, Adams's reaction to moral questions is physical and often violent; he dances at goodness, starts at vice. His morality operates not through introspection and analysis, but through natural instincts. Innocence, which is constantly ambushed by experience, reacts instinctively and violently, whereas worldliness relies on cunning and guile. Bruises are badges of courage.

In addition this violent vocabulary, like Joseph's defence of hunting, has the effect of giving goodness some muscle power. The combination of violence and virtue makes chastity *tough*. The fact that Fanny has a 'violent passion' for Joseph tells us that she is no pious hypocrite, but a woman with healthy, normal impulses: 'She loved with inexpressible violence, though with the purest and most delicate passion' (II, 10). This combination of toughness and tenderness, passion and chastity, violence and virtue, is precisely represented in the variable pressure of her embrace: 'which, tho' perhaps it would not have squeezed an insect to death, caused more emotion in the heart of Joseph, than the closest Cornish hug' (I, 11). Yet just a slight adjustment to this balance can turn a positive alliance into a satiric antithesis. For one of Fielding's favourite satiric effects is achieved by combining a violent physical adjective with a timid abstract noun. Typical examples are when Lady Booby attributes Joseph's bashfulness to 'the violent respect he preserves for her' (I, 5) or to his having 'too violent an awe and respect for herself' (IV, 1). Elsewhere the narrator ironically defers to the 'violent modesty' and 'rampant chastity' of his female readers (I, 8). In all these cases there is an obvious incongruity in the juxtaposition of physical adjectives with abstract nouns, and the resulting effect is satiric. Yet it is a kind of satire that comes perilously close to challenging the postures of the book's main characters. For surely Adams too is a violent defender of virtue, and Joseph and Fanny are both passionate champions of chastity.

By concentrating in this way on Fielding's use of violence, I do not wish to suggest any sombre subtext or Freudian nightmare lurking beneath the sunny surface of this comic novel. Claude Rawson has shown how Fielding's *Amelia* and other later novels reveal a crumbling of confidence in the Augustan ideals of virtue and good nature, with a correspondingly darker sense of the pervasive influence of hypocrisy and vice. But it would be false to pretend that such fears as these seriously discompose the cheerful optimism of *Joseph Andrews*. I simply wish to suggest that, in the blending of art and nature, a fine line separates a harmonious coalition from a hypocritical counterfeit. It is Fielding's comic tone which tells us on which side of that line he stands.

Once again then, what we have is a reminder of the dual tone of the novel: a duality balanced between the innocence of Adams and the urbanity of the narrator. Adams, Fanny and Joseph all embody a combination of violence and chastity in ways which carry no hint of irony, whereas the narrator instantly recognizes the ironigenic potential of such combinations, and offers us several examples in which the morality of the noun is merely a veil for the rapacity of the adjective.

Plot

The plot of *Tom Jones* has received considerable and well-justified praise, notably from Coleridge, who rated it alongside Sophocles's *Oedipus Tyrannus* and Jonson's *The Alchemist* as one of 'the three most perfect plots ever planned'. No one has ever said anything remotely like that about the plot of *Joseph Andrews*, though some of the disparagement of Fielding's narrative structure has been excessive. F. Holmes Dudden is typical of many critics when he describes *Joseph Andrews* as 'a tale of the picaresque type. The plan was not clearly thought out from the start, but almost seems to have been evolved extempore as the author proceeded.' As noted earlier, Fielding set himself something of a problem in plot terms with the ambiguous nature of his novel, part literary burlesque, part fictional comedy. The first ten chapters of *Joseph Andrews* form what is virtually a self-contained parody of *Pamela*. Even when Pamela herself appears in the final chapters of the novel, there is no real attempt to return to this original parodic style as a means of rounding the novel off. In fact, these first ten chapters can be regarded as a kind of satiric prelude or overture to the main comic plot. Thus Chapter 11, entitled 'Of Several New Matters Not Expected', gives us the feeling of a fresh start. Now, for the first time, we learn of the existence of Fanny, and from this point we are encouraged to see Joseph's chastity as an example of incorruptible fidelity, not of comic frigidity.

The plot of *Tom Jones* strikes us as peculiarly satisfying since it achieves a remarkable feat in blending art and nature together. While its structure proclaims the perfect symmetry of a work of art, its tone conveys the amiable leisurely freedom of a picaresque through inns and haystacks, the high road and the pleasant vales. Its eighteen books are carefully divided into three localized units: six in the country, six on the road and six in the town. Its mid-point, in the farcical scenes at the inn at Upton, contains the incident which appears to be Tom's moral nadir, when he believes himself to have committed incest with his mother; but it also marks the crucial shift in narrative momentum. Until that point Sophia had been chasing Tom; after this point, Tom is chasing her. The whole pattern of the novel charts the progress of a youth expelled from All-worthy's little Eden in Somerset, and who seeks Sophia (Greek for 'wisdom') in the city. This firm formal and allegorical structure prevents the adventures from appearing self-indulgent or repetitive, and lends all the amiable digressions an underlying sense of purpose.

The same cannot be said of *Joseph Andrews*, though there are some parallels. Martin Battestin has described the plot of the book as 'a moral pilgrimage from the vanity and corruption of the Great City to the relative naturalness and simplicity of the country'. The structure of the novel, he believes, 'despite incidental flaws, is not so haphazard, but rather consciously contrived and symmetrical'. There are indeed several parallels between the plot of *Joseph Andrews* and the story of the *Odyssey*, but, beyond doubt, the most important literary model for this novel is Cervantes's comic romance *Don Quixote*. Apart from the general similarities between the moral idealism of Parson Adams and Don Quixote, there are a number of parallel incidents and adventures which establish links between the two books. The night-time confusions involving Don Quixote, Maritornes and the mule-driver (*Don Quixote*, I, 16) might be compared with the misadventures in Slipslop's bed-chamber (IV, 14); the fright of Don Quixote and Sancho at the sight of strange lights (*Don Quixote*, I, 16) might be compared with the apprehensions of Adams, Joseph and Fanny when they see the lights of the sheep-stealers (III, 2); the practical jokes played by the Duke and Duchess on Don Quixote and Sancho (*Don Quixote*, II, 31) might be compared with the treatment of Adams by the 'roasting' squire (III, 7).

During his analysis of the *Iliad* Adams draws particular attention to the important artistic concept of unity, or *harmotton*, in a literary work, 'from which every incident arises, and to which every episode immediately relates' (III, 2). It is clear from this that at least in theory, if not in practice, Fielding was endeavouring to achieve such a classical unity. Beneath the rambling and apparently haphazard incidents and adventures of this comic epic in prose, there is evidence of certain underlying principles of both morality and organization.

The journey which Joseph Andrews undertakes is in the reverse direction from that of Tom Jones. Whereas Tom is banished from the country to find wisdom in the city, Joseph leaves the vices and temptations of the city to rediscover innocence and simplicity in the country with Fanny. Their travels follow similar routes around the Western circuit, though few of the locations are identified in this book. Yet there is little of the overt patterning of *Tom Jones*, and the overall sense of the narrative is episodic. The 'changeling' theme itself appears as something of an afterthought, and all the business of the gypsies, the strawberry birthmark and Gammer Andrews's story seems rather perfunctory. An alert reader will no doubt pick up the early clue that 'Mr Joseph Andrews, the hero of our ensuing history, was *esteemed* [my italics] to be the only son of Gaffer and Gammer Andrews' (I, 2). But there are no preparatory hints or ironies to convey any hint of the ambiguity of Fanny's origins. Fielding is even careless enough to make a mistake here, telling us that 'she was a poor girl, who had been formerly bred up in Sir John's family' (I, 11), when he actually means Sir Thomas's. There is a similar slip in the matter of Joseph's livery. In Chapter 10, at the end of the parodic prelude, Joseph ostentatiously strips off his livery, preparatory to quitting London and setting off for the country: ' . . . and having stript off his livery, was forced to borrow a frock and breeches of one of the servants'. This gesture is no doubt intended to parallel Pamela's triumphant symbolism in renouncing the borrowed robes of Mr B.'s deceased mother, and resuming her own homely garments, such as her 'round-ear'd ordinary cap' and 'home-spun gown and petticoat'. When Pamela surveys her new costume of humility in the glass, it produces one of the most memorable expressions of combined vanity and humility in Richardson's novel.

> I . . . looked about me in the glass, as proud as any thing. To say truth, I never liked myself so well in my life.
> O the pleasure of descending with ease, innocence, and resignation! Indeed there is nothing like it! An humble mind, I plainly see, cannot meet with any very shocking disappointment, let fortune's wheel turn round as it will. (*Pamela*, Letter 24)

Almost certainly this deliciously ambiguous blend of self-admiration and moral posturing would have appealed to Fielding's sense of irony. So Joseph too renounces the livery of deference in favour of simple, even comic clothes. Only apparently, he doesn't. For, in the very next chapter, it is Joseph's livery which catches the innkeeper's attention. 'Joseph had no sooner seated himself by the kitchen-fire, than Timotheus, observing his livery, began to condole the loss of his late master' (I, 11). These are small points, but they may be symptomatic of a lack of shaping design. In this novel, unlike *Tom Jones*, the various details and episodes do not build into a larger fictional whole. The reader is not required to amass clues or unravel allegorical hints. In *Joseph Andrews*, for the most part, the various episodes, adventures, interpolated tales and debates remain isolated exemplars devoted to certain common moral themes. The controlling unity resides in the narrator's tone rather than in the structure of events.

In the same way Joseph himself is made to undergo a number of sudden symbolic transformations. To begin with he is a parody of his 'sister' Pamela, and a modern version of the biblical Joseph. Then he is turned into the victim in the 'Good Samaritan' episode. Naturally these roles do not contradict each other morally; but neither do they allow the character of Joseph to develop in a coherent fictional manner. Parson Adams too has both literary and moral affinities with a number of distinguished forebears. In part he is modelled, as already noted, on Cervantes's romantic idealist Don Quixote; yet his character gains a further classical dignity by association with his beloved Aeschylus and Homer, and Adams himself appears as the modern counterpart of one of their wandering heroes. Most important, however, is the identification indicated by his Christian name, Abraham. Just as Joseph is compared with his biblical namesake, so Adams is, in a sense, a modern version of the great Old Testament patriarch. Isaac Barrow, a clergyman whose views had a clear influence on Fielding's thought, often used the figures of Joseph and Abraham in his sermons to signify the virtues of chastity and charity respectively. In one sermon Barrow declared that: 'In the story of our father Abraham, his benignity to strangers, and hospitableness, is remarkable among all his deeds of goodness, being propounded to us as a pattern and encouragement to the like practice.' In another sermon he added this: 'Did not Abraham even prefer the good of others before his own, when he gladly did quit his country, patrimony, friends and kindred, to pass his days in a wandering pilgrimage?' These symbolic associations remind us that as we read through the escapades of Joseph Andrews and Parson Adams, we are not witnessing merely the adventures of individuals, but exemplary re-enactions of enduring human myths which have found expression in both classical literature and Christian morality.

Read simply as a story, the novel's various scenes may appear both episodic and repetitive. There are the numerous fights and accidents, the frequent attempts on Fanny's virginity, and the repeated debates on vanity and charity with an assortment of lawyers, clerics and innkeepers. After a while a reader may cease to distinguish clearly between one episode and another, since both the events themselves and the language in which they are described have certain formulaic similarities. However, viewed as a series of variations upon certain key moral and satiric themes, these repetitions reveal a deeper exemplary purpose. They are illustrations of a common pattern, glosses on a central text.

Certain episodes stand out as both moral and structural set-pieces. The 'Good Samaritan' episode (I, 12) or Mr Wilson's narrative (III, 3) are good examples. Wilson's tale functions in much the same way as the interpolated tales in *Don Quixote*. It is a miniature 'rake's progress', a microcosmic warning of what might have befallen Joseph had he remained in London. It offers us, in one chapter, an epitome of the novel's theme. Martin Battestin describes it as 'the philosophic, as well as structural center of *Joseph Andrews*'. Indeed, Wilson's early enthusiasm to acquire a knowledge of the town is very similar to Joseph's own early naïve excitement for the place. Here is Wilson's account:

The character I was ambitious of attaining, was that of a fine gentleman; the first requisites to which, I apprehended were to be supplied by a tailor, a periwig-maker, and some few more tradesmen, who deal in furnishing out the human body ... The next qualifications, namely dancing, fencing, riding the great horse, and musick came into my head ... Knowledge of the town seemed another ingredient; this I thought I should arrive at by frequenting publick places. Accordingly I paid constant attendance to them all; by which means I was soon master of the fashionable phrases, learn'd to cry up the fashionable diversions, and knew the names and faces of the most fashionable men and women. (III, 3)

Here, to compare, is Joseph:

No sooner was young Andrews arrived at London, than he began to scrape an acquaintance with his party-colour'd brethren, who endeavour'd to make him despise his former course of life. His hair was cut after the newest fashion, and became his chief care. He went abroad with it all the morning in papers, and drest it out in the afternoon ... He applied most of his leisure hours to music, in which he greatly improved himself, and became so perfect a connoisseur in that art, that he led the opinion of all the other footmen at an opera, and they never condemned or applauded a single song contrary to his approbation or dislike. He was a little too forward in riots at the play-houses and assemblies: and when he attended his lady at church (which was but seldom) he behaved with less seeming devotion than formerly: however, he was outwardly a pretty fellow, his morals remained entirely uncorrupted, tho' he was at the same time smarter and genteeler, than any of the beaus in town, either in or out of livery. (I, 4)

Moreover, the providential conclusion of Wilson's tale, with its description of his 'golden age' life of retirement and domesticity, provides a model for Joseph and Fanny to imitate. At the heart of Wilson's tale is the moral distinction between an atheistical reliance on 'fortune' and a Christian faith in Providence. Wilson's real downfall begins when he becomes a gamester and, putting his trust in fortune, loses the remainder of his inheritance:

This opened scenes of life hitherto unknown; poverty and distress, with their horrid train of duns, attorneys, bailiffs, haunted me day and night. My clothes grew shabby, my credit bad, my friends and acquaintances of all kinds cold. (III, 3)

After descending the circles of this social hell from playwright to Grub Street hack, he finally buys a lottery ticket, 'resolving to throw myself into fortune's lap, and try if she would make me amends for the injuries she had done me at the gaming-table'. But he is forced to sell his ticket for a loaf of bread. Subsequently, when he learns that the ticket would have won him £3,000, he recognizes this as 'only a trick of fortune to sink me the deeper'. Imprisoned for debt, he has now 'neither health ... liberty, money or friends; and had abandoned all hopes and even the desire of life'. When Wilson is miraculously rescued from this state of desolation and despair by the charity and love of his future wife, Harriet Hearty, it may seem at first like merely another turn of fortune's wheel. But, in fact, it is Wilson's opportunity to escape from the gamester's treadmill of false hopes and vain ambitions by recognizing that his true hopes should repose in God's benign Providence. 'Sir,' he replies to Adams at the conclusion of his tale, 'I am thankful to the great author of all things for the blessings I here enjoy.'

I have several times already referred to Wilson's tale as a 'rake's progress' and the similarities between this story and Hogarth's series of paintings with that title, completed in 1733, is unmistakable. In the *Champion* (June 1740) Fielding wrote:

> I esteem the ingenious Mr Hogarth as one of the most useful satirists any age hath produced. In his excellent works you see the delusive scene exposed with all the force of humour, and, on casting your eyes on another picture, you behold the dreadful and fatal consequence. I almost dare affirm that those two works of his, which he calls the Rake's and the Harlot's Progress, are calculated more to serve the cause of virtue, and for the preservation of mankind, than all the folios of morality which have been ever written.

The early stages of Wilson's decline follow, step by step, the same route as Hogarth's Tom Rakewell. In the first painting of Hogarth's series we see the young heir already surrounded by tailors, attorneys and those who, in Wilson's phrase, 'deal in furnishing out the human body'. In the second scene we see him resplendent in his new fashionable clothes, at the centre of a circle of sycophantic practitioners of the 'polite' arts, listed by Wilson as 'dancing, fencing, riding the great horse, and musick'. Scene 3 shows Tom Rakewell, drunk and bleary, in a notorious Covent Garden brothel. This corresponds to the phase in Wilson's career which he describes thus: 'Covent-Garden was now the farthest stretch of my ambition, where I shone forth in the balconies at the play-houses, visited whores, made love to orange-wenches, and damned plays.' In the following painting Rakewell, now pale and sickly, is arrested for debt. The same ignominy befell Wilson who, having skulked and hidden in his garret lodging to avoid creditors, was finally caught by a bailiff disguised in women's clothing: 'He arrested me at my tailor's suit, for thirty-five pounds.' The real point of divergence between these two stories occurs with Hogarth's fifth painting in the series. At this point, whereas Wilson pins his hopes on a lottery ticket, Rakewell opts for the surer but more ignoble expedient of a marriage to a rich and ugly widow. Throughout the sequence of paintings Rakewell's progress is shadowed by the figure of the innocent young girl Sarah, whom he has seduced, and who bears his child. She represents many of the same values of innocent good nature embodied by Fanny in *Joseph Andrews* (though without her strict chastity). It is Rakewell's action now, rejecting her love and his child in favour of a loveless and mercenary marriage, which seals his fate. At the same point Wilson is finally redeemed through the love of a virtuous woman, Harriet Hearty, and restored to a happy life, free from vanity and affectation. Yet the parallels persist. Rakewell's gambling continues and brings him to the debtor's prison where he, like Wilson, tries to make some money as a playwright. No doubt this was a little satiric touch that Fielding would have relished. But the final scenes of the two stories provide us with two very different images of the consequences of the 'rake's progress'. Wilson, redeemed from vanity and restored to a life of peaceful tranquillity, is pictured as a reformed man, a patriarch of a new golden age. Rakewell, on the other hand, who could never shake off his gambler's addiction for trying another and yet another last throw of the dice, ends as a grotesque naked figure grovelling in chains on the floor of Bedlam. If Hogarth's *Rake's Progress* shows us the 'dreadful and fatal consequence' of vice, Fielding offers us the restorative of hope, with the Christian promise of salvation through love and forgiveness through charity. Hogarth's final scene is an image of Hell; Fielding reminds us that the repentant sinner can still hope to enjoy Paradise.

The other interpolated tales contained within *Joseph Andrews*, such as the story of Leonora (II, 4, 6) and the tale read by Adams's son Dick (IV, 10), work in a similar manner as self-contained moral exemplars. Though they appear to have little relation to the main narrative thrust of the novel, they offer interesting amplifications of the central themes of vanity and deception. In addition they also function in the plot as delaying devices. The story of Leonora, which encloses Adams's fight with Tow-wouse, provides a neat ironic frame for the 'horrible spectacle' of Adams all covered with hog's-blood. Similarly Dick's story of Paul and Leonard injects a little suspense by delaying the dénouement of the novel, while incidentally offering some advice on the value of candour in marriage.

Apart from these digressions, the main narrative follows a reliable if unsubtle pattern, alternating between scenes of slapstick action and scenes of moral and philosophical debate. Fielding has a particular fondness for what one might normally consider a rather theatrical device: the volte-face. Thus, when a character declares that all cowards should be hanged and talks with great warmth 'about courage and his country' (II, 9), we are not surprised to find him trembling with fright on the next page and running away from a noise in the bushes. When Adams offers 'philosophical observations on the folly of growing warm in disputes' (II, 11), we anticipate that in the next paragraph he will come to blows in a violent defence of his opinions. Or again, when Adams counsels Joseph to abstain from immoderate grief and to 'submit in all things to the will of Providence', we are instinctively prepared for the subsequent contradiction. Sure enough, shortly afterwards a messenger runs to tell Adams that his youngest son has drowned, and the parson proceeds to 'stamp about the room and deplore his loss with the bitterest agony' (IV, 8).

This characteristic volte-face device is a dramatized version of an irony that operates throughout the book, exposing the distinction between what is said and what is meant. The same irony can be seen in Fielding's subtle use of euphemism in the language of this novel, a subject to which I shall return later.

Fielding's Moral Outlook

For most of the time since the publication of *Joseph Andrews* Fielding's celebration of good nature, simplicity and charity in this novel has been regarded as a form of generalized genial optimism with little specifically philosophical or doctrinal basis. To the extent that his views were associated with any received philosophical theory, they have normally been identified with the 'benevolism' of Lord Shaftesbury's *Characteristics of Men, Manners, Opinions, and Times* (1711). Sir John Hawkins made this identification plain when he described Fielding's emphasis on natural goodness and social benevolism as the morality 'of Lord Shaftesbury vulgariz'd'. However, as others have shown, Fielding was in fact unhappy with the deistic tendencies implicit in much of Shaftesbury's thought, and more recent scholars have demonstrated that both the themes and the language of *Joseph Andrews* are deeply influenced by specific controversies and debates on matters of Christian doctrine within the Anglican Church. In the view of Martin Battestin, it is the liberal moralism of the lower clergy, rather than the principles of Cicero or Shaftesbury, that underlies the ethos and much of the art of *Joseph Andrews*. According to this view, Christian allegory is not confined to such isolated incidents as the 'Good Samaritan' episode or the story of Joseph and Potiphar's wife, but permeates the whole novel. In particular it is now clear that Fielding's moral outlook throughout the novel is deeply influenced by the writings of such latitudinarian clergymen as Isaac Barrow, John Tillotson, Samuel Clarke and Benjamin Hoadly. Latitudinarianism was a tendency within the Anglican Church which flourished at the beginning of the eighteenth century, largely as a reaction against the cynical materialism of Hobbes and the rigorous puritanism of the Calvinists. Central to the latitudinarian doctrine was a belief in the essential goodness of human nature, on the basis of which they formulated a religion of practical morality. It was an axiom of the latitudinarian position that a sincere man might gain salvation through charity and good works. Hence they hoped that the twin objects of social regeneration and individual salvation might be achieved through the exercise of charity. Benjamin Hoadly said in 1702:

> Did men but consider, that the great branch of Christian duty, is love, and good-nature, and humanity; and the distinguishing mark of a Christian, an universal charity; they could not but own that Jesus Christ came to plant and propagate them in the world. ('Of the Divisions, and Cruelties, Falsely Imputed to Christianity')

In a sermon on the Good Samaritan which evidently had an influence on *Joseph Andrews* Hoadly declared that 'the great and solemn audit to come turns all upon charity'. By charity he meant not only the giving of alms, but an active, positive benevolence, a genuine love of humanity. Isaac Barrow, in a sermon entitled 'The Duty and Reward of Bounty to the Poor', describes charity as a way of life, an attitude of heart and mind:

> Every thing, I say, which he hath in substance, or can do by his endeavour, that may conduce to the support of the life, or the health, or the welfare in any kind of his neighbour, to the succour or relief of his indigency, to the removal or easement of his affliction, he may well here be understood to disperse and give. Feeding the hungry, clothing the naked, visiting the sick, entertaining the stranger, ransoming the captive, easing the oppressed, comforting the sorrowful, assisting the weak, instructing or advising the ignorant, together with all such kinds or instances of beneficence, may be conceived . . . as the matter of the good man's dispersing and giving.

It is just such a principle of universal charity and benevolence that Adams represents.

This latitudinarian emphasis upon charity and good works led to a consequential downgrading of faith as the sole means of gaining salvation. 'A right faith is wholly in order to a good life, and is of no further value than it hath an influence upon it,' wrote Tillotson. 'The knowledge of religion is only in order to the practice of it; and an article or proposition of faith is an idle thing, if it do not produce such actions as the belief in such a proposition doth require.' Such ideas as this gained a wide currency in the literature of the period, which was anxious to escape from the theological dogmatism of the seventeenth century. In the *Spectator* Addison wrote that 'infidelity is not of so malignant a nature as immorality' and expressed his conviction that it was 'generally owned' that 'there may be salvation for a virtuous infidel (particularly in the case of invincible ignorance) but none for the vicious believer'. Hoadly's expression of this conviction, in his sermon on the Good Samaritan, is virtually copied by Adams. Here is Hoadly:

> We may be . . . certain that an honest heathen is much more acceptable to [God], than a dishonest and deceitful Christian; and that a charitable and good-natured pagan has a better title to his favour, than a cruel and barbarous Christian, let him be never so orthodox in his faith.

Adams gives his version of this belief when he informs the bookseller of his opinion: 'which hath always been, that a virtuous and good Turk, or heathen, are more acceptable in the sight of their Creator, than a vicious and wicked Christian, tho' his faith was as perfectly orthodox as St Paul's himself' (I, 17). In his essay 'On the Knowledge of the Characters of Men' Fielding makes explicit his own adherence to a morality based on good works rather than faith, deeds rather than words. 'Surely the actions of men seem to be the justest interpreters of their thoughts, and the truest standards by which we may judge them,' he writes. 'By their fruits you shall know them, is a saying of great wisdom, as well as authority.'

However, the latitudinarians did not have things all their own way, and with the Methodist revival in the late 1730s preachers like George Whitefield and John Wesley renewed the Calvinist insistence on faith as man's only means of salvation. In a sermon preached in 1740 Whitefield poured scorn on the idea that a human being could earn salvation through good works:

> For salvation is the free gift of God. I know no fitness in man, but a fitness to be cast into the lake of fire and brimstone for ever. Our righteousnesses in God's sight are but as filthy rags: he cannot away with them.

And, in a letter the previous year, he wrote:

> We must not expect to be saved, or any way recommend ourselves to God, by any or all the works of righteousness which we have done, or shall, or can do. The Lord Christ is our righteousness – our whole righteousness: imputed to us, instead of our own ... Christ bought our justification with a great price, even with his own blood. It comes to us freely, without any regard to works past, present, or to come.

In his doctrinal dispute with Barnabas (I, 17) Adams takes specific issue with Whitefield's beliefs, calling the doctrine of justification by faith as opposed to good works a 'detestable' theory. In his view it amounts to no more than a kind of theological hypocrisy, which would allow a Christian villain to plead before the Last Judgement 'Lord, it is true I never obeyed one of thy commandments, yet punish me not, for I believe them all.'

Among the various latitudinarian divines, the one whose influence upon *Joseph Andrews* appears to have been greatest was Isaac Barrow. It was from Barrow's sermons that Fielding seems to have derived the idea of giving the names Abraham and Joseph to his two heroic examples of Christian charity and chastity. As already noted, in his sermons on 'The Love of Our Neighbour' and on 'The Duty and Reward of Bounty to the Poor' Barrow used the figure of Abraham as a model of selfless benevolence and charity. In another sermon 'Of the Virtue and Reasonableness of Faith' Barrow cites Joseph's resistance of the advances of Potiphar's wife as an example of virtue triumphing over temptation. But Fielding seems to have been particularly inspired by Barrow's sermon 'Of Being Imitators of Christ'. There, Barrow begins with some observations on the power of example which evidently influenced Fielding's narrator's remarks on the same subject in the first chapter of *Joseph Andrews*. Here is Barrow:

> Examples do more compendiously, easily, and pleasantly inform our minds, and direct our practice, than precepts, or any other way of instrument or discipline.

Here, to compare, is Fielding:

> It is a trite but true observation, that examples work more forcibly on the mind than precepts: and if this be just in what is odious and blameable, it is more strongly so in what is amiable and praiseworthy. Here emulation most effectually operates upon us, and inspires our imitation in an irresistible manner.

In particular, Barrow goes on, the lives of the patriarchs in 'the divine histories' offer 'patterns of virtue and piety' which are of greater value than any amount of sermons, since 'one good example may represent more fully and clearly to us the nature of a virtue, than any verbose description thereof can do'.

In adapting and modernizing the figure of Abraham, translating him from the world of scripture to the world of comic romance, Fielding recasts simple Christian parables in a fictional form acceptable to a sophisticated readership. As he writes in the first chapter:

> But as it often happens that the best men are but little known, and consequently cannot extend the usefulness of their examples a great way; the writer may be called in aid to spread their history farther, to present the amiable pictures to those who have not the happiness of knowing the originals; and so, by communicating such valuable patterns to the world, may perhaps do a more extensive service to mankind than the persons whose life originally afforded the pattern.

While it would be a piece of absurd hubris for Fielding to imply that his Parson Adams might be better known, or offer a 'more extensive service to mankind', than the figure of Abraham, he may accurately surmise that his comic novel might reach an audience which seldom or never troubled itself with the Bible. He offers us a modern Abraham, and cleverly packages his moral idealism with an attractive wrapping of social comedy and literary burlesque.

As one reads further in Barrow's sermon 'Of Being Imitators of Christ', its influence upon *Joseph Andrews* becomes unmistakable. For the two prime examples from 'the divine histories' which Barrow cites are Abraham, the model of true faith, and Joseph, the pattern of chastity. He describes how Abraham willingly leaves his dear native land, 'his estate and patrimony, his kindred and acquaintance, to wander he knew not where in unknown lands ... leading an uncertain and ambulatory life in tents, sojourning and shifting among strange people, devoid of piety and civility, (among Canaanites and Egyptians) . . .' Parson Adams leads just such an 'uncertain and ambulatory life' as this, and the strangers that he meets sometimes strike him as the equivalents of Canaanites and Egyptians. 'He almost began to suspect that he was sojourning in a country inhabited only by Jews and Turks' (II, 16). Similarly Barrow's description of Joseph's situation in Potiphar's household offers a close parallel with Joseph Andrews's awkward plight in the early chapters of the novel:

> . . . rejecting the solicitations of an imperious mistress, advantaged by opportunities of privacy and solitude; when the refusal was attended with extreme danger, and all the mischiefs, which the disdain of a furious lust disappointed, of an outrageous jealousy provoked . . . ,

When the full range of these careful parallels is recognized, the plot of *Joseph Andrews* comes to seem less like a random sequence of picaresque adventures, and takes on the form of a moral pilgrimage away from the city of temptations, towards the relative innocence and simplicity of the country.

In his essay 'On the Knowledge of the Characters of Men' Fielding addresses himself directly to the moral conundrum which underlies much of his fiction. This is that those moral qualities which he most prized, such as innocence, good nature and benevolence, are the very qualities which disable a good man from distinguishing and defending against the wiles and stratagems of hypocrites and knaves. 'That open disposition, which is the surest indication of an honest and upright heart, chiefly renders us liable to be imposed on by craft and deceit, and principally disqualifies us for this discovery . . . It will be difficult for honest and undesigning men to escape the snares of cunning and imposition.' It is one of Fielding's chief aims in his writing to stand up as a champion of the innocent and undesigning, and to 'arm them against imposition'. For, although 'the whole world becomes a vast masquerade, where the greatest part appear disguised under false vizors and habits', yet he retains a belief that nature 'is ever endeavouring to peep forth and shew herself'. The hypocrite is never so accomplished in his deceit, but that some natural failing in his manner, language, physiognomy or behaviour will betray his true character. 'However cunning the disguise be which a masquerader wears . . . he very rarely escapes the discovery of an accurate observer.' Parson Adams, we know, is forever unable to distinguish the cunning traps of the hypocrites and villains who beset him, but Fielding's moral purpose is not to educate Adams, but to caution us. He gives us at the same time a model of moral idealism and a gazetteer of social temptations. By combining the two he endeavours to offer us both an inspiring example to warm our hearts and a warning to sharpen our observation.

As is obvious from the whole tone and outlook of *Joseph Andrews*, Fielding took a generally optimistic view of human nature. In *Tom Jones* (IV, 1) he condemned 'that modern doctrine that there was no such things as virtue or goodness really existing in human nature, and ... deduced our best actions from pride'. Clearly he has in mind the theories of such writers as Hobbes, Mandeville and La Rochefoucauld. As a reformer, first as a writer and subsequently as a magistrate, Fielding sought to promote the good examples which would enshrine the natural propensity to virtue and discourage the temptations of vice. In *Amelia* Dr Harrison remarks:

> The nature of man is far from being in itself evil; it abounds with benevolence, charity and pity, coveting praise and honour, and shunning shame and disgrace. Bad education, bad habits and bad customs debauch our nature, and direct it headlong as it were, into vice. (IX, 5)

Hence throughout *Joseph Andrews* we find a considerable emphasis placed on education and moral examples as encouragements for this natural sense of goodness. Wilson imputes all his later misfortunes to his 'early introduction into life without a guide'. His liberal education had been quite insufficient to prepare him to withstand the temptations of the world, a fact which comes as no surprise to Adams who views such schools as 'the microcosms of all vice and immorality' (III, 5). Turning to Joseph, he remarks, 'You may thank the Lord you were not bred at a public school, you would never have preserved your virtue as you have.'

Joseph's reply, however, has a significance which goes beyond the debate between the respective merits of a public school or private education. Having reminded Adams, with all due deference, that Sir Thomas Booby's morals had suffered no corruption at public school, and that 'several country gentlemen who were educated within five miles of their own houses ... are as wicked as if they had known the world from their infancy', Joseph draws this conclusion:

> I remember when I was in the stable, if a young horse was vicious in his nature, no correction would make him otherwise; I take it to be equally the same among men: if a boy be of a mischievous wicked inclination, no school, tho' ever so private, will ever make him good; on the contrary, if he be of a righteous temper, you may trust him to London, or wherever else you please, he will be in no danger of being corrupted. (III, 5)

This conclusion echoes the view which Fielding himself took in his essay 'On the Knowledge of the Characters of Men'. There he describes certain original and apparently innate differences between the characters of different individuals:

> This original difference will, I think, alone account for that very early and strong inclination to good or evil, which distinguishes different dispositions in children in their first infancy ... and in persons who from the same education &c might be thought to have directed nature the same way; yet among all these, there subsists, as I have before hinted, so manifest and extreme a difference of inclination or character, that almost obliges us, I think, to acknowledge some unacquired, original distinction, in the nature or soul of one man, from that of another.

Only such an original distinction could account for the situation which we encounter in *Tom Jones*. Tom and Blifil have both been raised in the same house and undergone the same education, but while Tom has retained his warm-hearted good nature, Blifil is a scheming hypocrite. Indeed, the two are presented to us as a perfect moral antithesis. Whatever Blifil does, and however noble the motivation which he claims, we always know him to be selfish and mean-spirited, whereas Tom, no matter what scrapes he gets into, is always generous and kind. So clear-cut and irredeemable does this division between them appear that some critics have accused Fielding of presenting a quasi-Calvinist distinction between the fallen and the chosen. Yet this would fly in the face of Fielding's explicit belief in the doctrine of good works, and his faith in the efficacy of moral examples. It is clear that Fielding never arrived at a satisfactory resolution of this dilemma, since if human beings are 'vicious by nature' then neither moral education nor social satire can have any hope of reforming them. In the *Champion* (December 1739) he wrote: 'Though I am unwilling to look on human nature as a mere sink of iniquity, I am far from insinuating that it is a state of perfection.' As he grew older, his experiences as a magistrate led him to reflect in a more melancholy vein on the apparently ineradicable elements of evil in some human natures. Considering the sad case of the abducted girl Elizabeth Canning, he wrote:

> How many cruelties, indeed, do we daily hear of, to which it seems not easy to assign any other motive than barbarity itself? In serious and sorrowful truth, doth not history, as well as our own experience, afford us too great reasons to suspect, that there is in some minds a sensation directly opposite to that of benevolence, and which delights and feeds itself with acts of cruelty and inhumanity?

For the most part, however, Fielding appears to have consoled himself with the belief that those in whom this innate delight in acts of cruelty manifested itself represented only a small proportion of humanity. The majority of mankind was composed of people whose natural instincts of benevolence might be inspired by the example of virtue and warmed by the comic exposure of affectation.

As we have seen, charity is the cardinal virtue in the system of Christian benevolence presented in *Joseph Andrews*. Adams's dispute with Barnabas (I, 17) displays the theoretical distinction between the rival doctrines of justification by faith or by good works. But his argument with the hog-farmer and Sunday parson Trulliber indicates the practical differences, in matters of charity, that flow from these two positions. Asked by Adams for a loan of fourteen shillings, Trulliber is thrown into a frenzy of indignation, and declares, 'I know what charity is, better than to give it to vagabonds.' Adams is sorry to hear Trulliber's claim that he knows what charity is, 'since you practise it no better'. He goes on:

'I must tell you, if you trust to your knowledge for your justification, you will find yourself deceived, tho' you should add faith to it without good works.' 'Fellow,' cries Trulliber, 'Dost thou speak against faith in my house? Get out of my doors ...' (II, 14)

Once again we are encouraged to see the doctrine of justification by faith as the purest hypocrisy, allowing Trulliber to preach the virtue of charity while behaving like an avaricious and mean-spirited miser. 'There is no command more express, no duty more frequently enjoined than charity,' declares Adams in orthodox latitudinarian style. 'Whoever therefore is void of charity, I make no scruple of pronouncing that he is no Christian' (II, 14).

Two chapters later Adams encounters another form of hypocritical charity, in the person of the liberal stranger at the inn who showers him with promises of board, lodging and a living. Adams is overcome with gratitude. 'Blessed be the hour which first introduced me to a man of your charity. You are indeed a Christian of the true primitive kind' (II, 16). However, we quickly discover that the promises are mere words; the stranger disappears, leaving Adams and his companions actually worse off than when they met him. 'What wickedness is there in the Christian world?' exclaims Adams at this apparently motiveless exercise in malicious deception.

Most often in social conversations, charity, like those other awkward moral terms, honour and virtue, is used as a euphemism for a form of self-interest. For example, an 'honest elderly man' offers 'out of pure charity' to arrange a duel between Mr Wilson and a captain of the guards. 'A very charitable person, truly!' observes Adams (III, 3).

Adams's own definition of charity, addressed to Peter Pounce, is characteristically simple: 'a generous disposition to relieve the poor', yet not so simple but that the casuistical Pounce can find a way of agreeing with its form, while denying its force:

> 'There is something in that definition,' answered Peter, 'which I like well enough; it is, as you say, a disposition – and does not so much consist in the act as in the disposition to do it; but alas, Mr Adams, who are meant by the distressed? Believe me, the distresses of mankind are mostly imaginary, and it would be rather folly than goodness to relieve them.' (III, 13)

Peter Pounce is a satirical portrait of the notorious miser Peter Walter, a dishonest steward from Fielding's own home territory in Dorset who, through a sustained policy of extortion, peculation and money-lending, had acquired a fortune of some £200,000. Here Pounce is revealed as another hypocrite who prefers theory to practice, and who can applaud the idea of charity so long as he is not expected to put his hand into his pocket. To him charity must always be an abstraction since the hardships and distresses of the world are themselves merely imaginary. When Adams protests that hunger, thirst, cold and nakedness can hardly be considered imaginary conditions, Pounce has a ready answer:

> 'How can any man complain of hunger,' said Peter, 'in a country where such excellent sallads are to be gathered in almost every field? or of thirst, where every river and stream produces such delicious potations?' (III, 13)

The modern reader should not be misled here by our late-twentieth-century fashion for high-fibre diets and salads into associating this with Parson Adams's fondness for simple meals of bread and cheese and ale. Pounce is revealed here as the worst kind of miser: a sanctimonious hypocrite who disguises his avarice as a philosophical system. This high-minded asceticism, as Fielding goes on to demonstrate, comes from the mouth of a man who cannot resist boasting of his own avaricious skills in amassing a fortune of at least £40,000. And were it not, as he points out, for the 'vice of good nature', he would hardly suffer so shabby a person as Adams to share his coach. At which Adams, declining to presume further on the strained quality of Pounce's charity, leaps from the coach in disgust.

It might be interesting to compare the various casuistical evasions and perversions of the Christian duty of charity revealed in *Joseph Andrews* with a passage from Pope's satiric *Epistle to Lord Bathurst*, published in 1733 and subtitled 'Of the Use of Riches'. Not only does Pope cite Peter Walter as a prime target for attack in this poem, he also deftly exposes many of the same hollow excuses that Fielding's characters express:

> *Perhaps you think the poor might have their part?*
> *Bond damns the poor, and hates them from his heart:*
> *The grave Sir Gilbert holds it for a rule,*
> *That 'every man in want is knave or fool:'*
> *'God cannot love (says Blunt, with tearless eyes)*
> *The wretch he starves' – and piously denies:*
> *But the good bishop, with a meeker air,*
> *Admits, and leaves them Providence's care.*
> 　*Yet, to be just to these poor men of pelf,*
> *Each does but hate his neighbour as himself:*
> *Damn'd to the mines, an equal fate betides*
> *The slave that digs it, and the slave that hides.*

Bond here is Denis Bond, a director of the Charitable Corporation for the Relief of Industrious Poor, who was found guilty of embezzling corporation funds, retorting 'Damn the poor!' But Pope also uses his name in a semi-metaphorical manner, transforming him into a personification of the world of stocks and bonds, and a symbol of the bondage and tyranny of avarice. The repeated monosyllables in the line are like repeated hammer blows, and Bond's instinctive callousness is emphasized by the alliterative antithesis of 'hates them from his heart'. Yet his brutality is frank and undisguised; his meanness has at least the virtue of honesty, contrasted with the hypocritical cant of 'Sir Gilbert', who pretends to justify his lack of charity with a convenient philosophical platitude. Blunt indulges a similar vein of sophistry to defend his meanness, but whereas Sir Gilbert merely invokes his own brand of natural-law philosophy, Blunt goes further and claims a divine right and precedent for his miserly behaviour. Pope's specific target here is Sir John Blunt, but as with Bond he exploits this monosyllabic name as a symbol for a harsh bluntness or callousness of heart. That cunning parenthesis, 'with tearless eyes', is a masterly ironic touch, raising the suggestion of tearfulness only to deny it, and thus confirming the bluntness of Blunt. The others too, one imagines, have tearless eyes, but Pope finds it unnecessary to tell us so. More importantly, Blunt's belief that 'God cannot love ...' is a direct contradiction of the New Testament message that God is love, and indicates the subtle anti-Christian crescendo, starting with Bond's 'damn' that animates this passage. That final, sly formulation, 'and piously denies', beautifully encapsulates the kind of hypocritical casuistry that preserves the language of Christianity while inverting its meaning. At first the bishop is presented as a complete contrast with all that has gone before, but, in fact, we soon see that the distinction is of a theoretical, not a practical, kind. Whereas Blunt believes that God punishes wrong-doers by starving them, and thus that it would be condoning sin to relieve their suffering, the bishop takes a different view of the role of Providence. In his view God can be relied upon to take care of the poor and needy, which conveniently absolves the rich from any necessity to do so. He is a perfect example of the theory of justification by faith.

At this point Pope's own voice intrudes in judgemental tones to draw attention to the deliberate pattern of inverted Christian imagery running through the passage.

> *Yet, to be just to these poor men of pelf,*
> *Each does but hate his neighbour as himself:*

That oxymoron 'poor men of pelf' ('pelf' means wealth) points up the ironic contrast between material poverty and poverty of spirit. The absence of charity which leads Blunt to deny God's love returns to plague him in a world where counting has replaced compassion and hate has taken the place of love. Picking up Bond's initial 'damn the poor', Pope shows that it is Bond himself who is damned by his own callousness: 'Damn'd to the mines . . .' The mines here have two meanings. In a physical sense they are the gold or coal mines where the poor are condemned to labour for the enrichment of others. But they are also the mines of Hell, whither those like Bond, Blunt and Sir Gilbert, who have led unchristian, uncharitable lives, will be damned for all eternity. This equal fate has both a comic and a tragic face. Comically, Pope offers a mirror image: one of a literal slave, labouring to dig the gold from the earth; while the other, a slave to his own greed, buries the gold away again in vaults underground. In tragic terms the cupidity which will take these misers to Hell condemns the poor to a hell on earth for all their mortal lives.

I have dwelt on this passage at some length because Pope's central contention in this poem, that money has replaced love as the dynamic principle in social and moral relationships, is one which Fielding shares, and which has a great importance in *Joseph Andrews*. Among the various attitudes to charity which we find expressed in this novel, Mrs Towwouse's direct contempt offers a rough parallel with Bond's response. 'Common charity, a f—t!' says she, 'common charity teaches us to provide for ourselves and our families' (I, 12). Peter Pounce, on the other hand, has the casuistical evasiveness of Sir Gilbert, while Trulliber demonstrates the pious callousness of Blunt. All of them, however, in matters of money have a roughness of expression avoided by Pope's more patrician misers. Peter Pounce, for example, tells Adams that he cares 'not a fig, no not a fart' for his opinion (III, 13).

Perhaps the closest parallel with this passage from Pope's poem to be found in *Joseph Andrews* comes in the 'Good Samaritan' episode, where Fielding similarly exposes a number of individual reactions to the issue of charity (I, 12). The lady disguises meanness as morality, turning Joseph's nakedness into an occasion for horror, not compassion. 'O *J-sus*,' cry'd the lady, 'A naked man! Dear coachman, drive on . . .' Here, as in the Pope passage, the Christian language ('J-sus') is a nice ironic touch, revealing her Christianity as a formulaic trope, rather than a living moral force. The gentleman is motivated by a form of prudence which sees no link between self-interest and social responsibility. 'Robbed,' cries an old gentleman. 'Let us make all the haste imaginable, or we shall be robbed too.' The lawyer, as one might expect, is the perfect casuist, and understands responsibility strictly in its legalistic, not its moral, sense: 'He therefore thought it advisable to save the poor creature's life, for their own sakes, if possible.' Only the postillion is in any way moved by a feeling of common humanity or compassion for Joseph's plight and he, as we are informed in a satiric aside, 'hath been since transported for robbing a hen-roost'. Fielding uses this little comic vignette to show how the various codes and rules – legal, financial, social – by which society is held together can be used as convenient pretexts for evading the moral responsibilities of a shared humanity. Each character has his or her own scrap or trope of formal self-justification to indemnify them against contamination by feelings of compassion, benevolence or love.

Fielding's moral values in *Joseph Andrews* are thus perfectly clear, but of course a comic novel is not the same thing as a moral treatise; and a picaresque arrangement of social parables and moral essays does not necessarily result in a satisfying work of fiction. Naturally, this is not the same as demanding that *Joseph Andrews* should have a strict formal symmetry or unity of plot. 'To demand strict organic unity of the tales in eighteenth-century fiction,' writes Pat Rogers in *The Augustan Vision*, 'is like asking of an after-dinner speaker that his anecdotes should all have a common base.' Yet the creation of a work of fiction with characters and a plot inevitably raises the expectation that the moral issues in that work will largely be resolved in terms of these key ingredients. Quite often, however, readers may be left wondering how seriously Fielding wishes to insist upon his ideals of good nature and simplicity when characters are frequently only rescued from the consequences of their imprudent behaviour through the providential intervention of the narrator. Just as Providence, in the benevolent and wealthy form of Harriet Hearty, intervenes to save Wilson from destruction, so a comic plot and a good deal of mock-Homeric irony protect Adams from the consequences of his simple-hearted idealism. Ford Madox Ford had no patience with this kind of narrative contrivance which, in both *Tom Jones* and *Joseph Andrews*, has the effect of isolating characters from the consequences of their actions and providing a happy ending in the teeth of our experience of the world. Writing, admittedly, with *Tom Jones* rather than *Joseph Andrews* in mind, he denounced

fellows like Fielding ... who pretend that if you are a gay drunkard, lecher, squanderer of your goods, and fumbler in placket holes, you will eventually find a benevolent uncle, concealed father, or benefactor who will shower on you bags of ten thousands of guineas, estates, and the hands of adorable mistresses – these fellows are dangers to the body politic and horribly bad constructors of plots.

While it may be perfectly acceptable in romance for the pauper hero to be revealed as a prince and the ragged heroine as a princess, such endings may appear less appropriate in a satiric work which also includes some acute attacks on social affectations. The central problem really is the one which Fielding outlined in his essay 'On the Knowledge of the Characters of Men', namely that 'it will be difficult for honest and undesigning men to escape the snares of cunning and imposition'. How seriously can we take the moral idealism of Adams when it takes the practised, urbane insights of the narrator to see through the hypocrites whom he encounters on his travels? The same question is raised in *Tom Jones*. Tom is full of good-natured generosity and humanity, but his lack of prudence and circumspection are continually landing him in trouble. In Book V of *Tom Jones* Allworthy offers this assessment of Tom's character, which many critics have taken as a key statement of the novel's theme:

Allworthy then gently squeezed his hand, and proceeded thus. 'I am convinced, my child, that you have much goodness, generosity and honour in your temper; if you will add prudence and religion to these, you must be happy: for the three former qualities, I admit, make you worthy of happiness, but they are the latter only which will put you in possession of it.' (*Tom Jones*, V, 7)

Several commentators have presented the theme of 'prudence' as a central preoccupation of the novel. According to this view, Tom gradually learns through his experiences and misadventures to temper his instinctive generosity with a more prudent circumspection, and begins to use his head as well as his heart. While there is much to recommend this interpretation, there is also a good deal to be said against it. In particular there is the fact that 'prudence' and 'prudent' are favourite social euphemisms which Fielding loves to expose, and one scholar has calculated that in *Tom Jones* these words are used unfavourably three times as often as they are used favourably. The same is true of *Joseph Andrews*. There, if a character is described as 'prudent', or showing 'prudence', it is the narrator's ironic manner of telling us that he or she is a hypocrite. Leonora's aunt comments that 'the world is always on the side of prudence' (II, 4), by which she means greed, since this is her way of encouraging her niece to reject Horatio, who drives a pair of horses, in favour of Bellarmine, who drives six. When the narrator of the story of Leonora remarks how men of a fierce and courageous countenance will, if faced with the prospect of battle, 'prudently decline it', the word is a signal of cowardice. The same cowardly spirit animates the poet sent with the captain, the player and three servants to abduct Fanny; when confronted by Joseph, he 'prudently retreated downstairs, saying it was his business to record great actions, and not to do them'. Rather more sympathetic is the description of Parson Adams's wife as 'one of those prudent people who never do anything to injure their families' (IV, 8). Yet it is clear from the context here that her prudence, though inspired by the best of motives, is in fact a form of timidity which leads her to capitulate before Lady Booby's attempts to blackmail Adams into forbidding the marriage of Fanny and Joseph. Indeed, it is only a little removed from the attitude of Mrs Tow-wouse, who would confine charity to her own family. Fielding clearly endorses Adams's much wider understanding of charity: the parson views the whole of humanity as his family. The result of this universal love is seen on his welcome return to the parish. As soon as he appears, the whole village runs to greet him.

They flocked about him like dutiful children round an indulgent parent, and vyed with each other in demonstrations of duty and love. The parson on his side shook everyone by the hand, enquiring heartily after the healths of all that were absent, of their children and relations, and exprest a satisfaction in his face, which nothing but benevolence made happy by its objects could infuse. (IV, 1)

This reception is in marked contrast with the welcome given to Lady Booby, which is the result of money, not love. The parishioners 'rejoiced to see their patroness returned after so long an absence, during which time all her rents had been drafted to London, without a shilling being spent among them'.

Prudence, then, is usually a negative quality. It is the cautionary restraint of self-interest which checks the natural impulses of good nature. It proceeds from the head rather than the heart, and in Fielding's characters the division between 'good' and 'bad' often corresponds with this ana-tomical dichotomy. Heartfree and Hearty are typical names chosen to distinguish good, generous, benevolent characters, whereas characters like Blifil and Thwackum, Trulliber and Slipslop operate acording to a cold prudential calculus of self-interest.

Moreover, the two-dimensionality of these characters means that there is little possibility of psychological change or development within them. They are not so much changed as tested by the obstacles that beset them. The important thing is that their moral values, like their chastity, should remain intact. Characters are determined by the narrator's tone, and a figure once labelled 'prudent' can no more become good natured than a warm spontaneous character can become cold and calculating. The adjectives, however ironic, are definitive, and the behaviour of these characters is not naturalistic but exemplary. Richardson's characters, by contrast, are exemplary by virtue of their capacity for moral struggle. Clarissa's values remain pure and constant, but her psychology and spiritual self-awareness both undergo a variety of significant transformations. The nearest thing that one finds in *Joseph Andrews* is the comic oscillation of passions in the breast of Lady Booby.

> 'Whither doth this violent passion hurry us? What meannesses do we submit to from its impulse? Wisely we resist its first and least approaches; for it is then only we can assure ourselves the victory. No woman could ever safely say, *so far only will I go*. Have I not exposed myself to the refusal of my footman? I cannot bear the reflection.' (I, 8)

Yet this is little more than histrionic posturing, a piece of literary burlesque, which plays with these eddying waves of her ruling passion. In fact, the representation of this to-and-fro motion of her mind is no less formulaic than the alternating colour of her cheeks, flushing red and draining white: 'After some silence and a double change of her complexion; first to pale and then to red, she thus spoke' (IV, 6).

In his *Journey from This World to the Next* Fielding acknowledged that human beings were, of course, neither wholly good nor wholly bad, but varying blends in between. He imagined a pre-natal laboratory in Elysium where each spirit is required to drink from two phials. The first of these, the 'Pathetic Potion', is 'a mixture of all the passions, but in no exact proportion, so that sometimes one predominates and sometimes another'. The other phial, entitled the 'Nousphoric Decoction', is the source of the rational faculties. Fielding's characters then are intended to represent a blend of rational and passionate ingredients in a range of different human cocktails. In practice, however, the predominance of one faculty over the other is usually total. A 51 per cent majority representation for either ingredient is sufficient to make a character either violently good natured or prudently hypocritical. There is no proportional representation in

Masterstudies: Joseph Andrews

Fielding's characterization. The true blending of human nature is achieved not within any one individual character but within the novel as a whole. Parson Adams, Fanny and Joseph may be taken to represent the virtues of the 'Pathetic Potion', while the narrator, with his classical devices and urbane tone, embodies the 'Nousphoric Decoction' of rationality.

In his endeavour to act as a champion for the 'innocent and undesigning part of mankind', Fielding is never blind to the dangers and vulnerabilities of moral idealism. Indeed, he insistently draws attention to the buffetings and humiliations endured by Adams in his defence of innocence. And he reminds us that even in an idyllic pastoral retreat, dogs are killed and hares are hunted. *Joseph Andrews* does not offer us a vision of arcadia, but a glimpse of a life of relative simplicity, in which men consider it more honest to defend themselves with cudgels than with lies. Fielding offers us images and examples, not a manifesto. His novel breathes the inspiration of good-natured comedy rather than the studied ideas of dogmatic philosophy.

All of which brings us to the matter of chastity. One reason why readers may feel that Fielding is less than wholeheartedly committed to the ideal of chastity is that this too is a form of prudence, a restraint upon natural impulses. Virginity and virtue, or 'vartue' as it is termed in *Shamela*, are hypocritical euphemisms that have little to do with real morality, and much more to do with social hypocrisy. Throughout *Shamela* Fielding deftly parodies Pamela's obsessive fascination with the subject of her own virtue, turning this self-regard into a form of sanctimonious and hypocritical narcissism. 'And so we talked a full hour and a half, about my vartue,' remarks Shamela, artfully converting Pamela's moral qualms into a knowing ploy of sexual teasing. Even when not seen in this hypocritical light, chastity seems at best a negative quality, a denial of those natural impulses and instincts upon whose goodness Fielding puts so much emphasis. Thus the good nature of Betty the chambermaid has much in common with the generous vitality of Tom Jones.

She had good-nature, generosity and compassion, but unfortunately her constitution was composed of those warm ingredients, which, though the purity of courts and nunneries might have happily controuled them, were by no means able to endure the ticklish situation of a chamber-maid at an inn . . .(I, 18)

These warm impulses of natural generosity and spontaneity are precisely the qualities that Fielding's morality seems to celebrate. They are the instincts which provoke Adams to dance and caper at goodness, and which animate Tom Jones's love of life. In his introduction to the Penguin Edition of *Joseph Andrews*, R. F. Brissenden argues that the contrast between Betty and Mrs Tow-wouse 'is integral to the first part of the novel'. Whereas Mrs Tow-wouse's retort to her husband's suggestion that common charity requires them to help the injured Joseph is 'Common charity, a f—t!' (I, 12), Betty instinctively offers immediate aid. She warms Joseph by the fire, puts him to bed and runs 'with all speed to hasten the surgeon'. She herself had previously required the care of a surgeon to cool the flame raised in her by a visiting ensign of foot. But though a little wayward, particularly in the matter of chastity, Betty is definitely a 'good' character, just as Tom, who shares the same weakness, is essentially honest and generous. Add to this the fact that throughout the first ten chapters of the novel the word 'virtue' is used consistently in an ironic manner and we begin to see something of Fielding's dilemma. The concept of male virtue seems particularly comic. When Lady Booby declares 'Did ever mortal hear of a man's virtue!' (I, 8), the comedy partly resides in our recognition of the incongruity of this concept. Instinctively we sense that Fielding's sympathy is for the natural red-blooded animal spirits of Tom Jones, rather than for the priggish ideal of male virtue which all too easily resembles a form of pious Richardsonian cant. In the *Champion* (March 1740) Fielding warned against allowing even 'virtue itself' to become 'too exuberant ... Men often become ridiculous ... by over-acting even a laudable part.'

Yet it would be wrong to minimize the significance of chastity – even of male chastity – in Fielding's morality. In his play *The Wedding Day* the characteristically named Heartfort offers an important statement of sexual morality. While confessing that his practice may not always have measured up to his theories, he affirms, hand on heart, 'I never seduced a young woman to her own ruin, nor a married one to the misery of her husband.' He condemns the double-standards which 'make it infamous for women to grant what it is honourable for us to solicit'. Tom Jones too, though promiscuous, is never selfish or malicious.

'Lookee, Mr Nightingale,' said Jones, 'I am no canting hypocrite, nor do I pretend to the gift of chastity more than my neighbours. I have been guilty with women, I own it; but am not conscious that I have ever injured any. Nor would I, to procure pleasure to myself, be knowingly the cause of misery to any human being.'

The reason – or at least one possible reason – why male virtue may seem comic is that virginity in men, unlike in women, conferred no social status or economic value. For Pamela, as Fielding's *Shamela* wickedly exposes, virginity is a material asset, and hence her defence of her chastity may be seen as a triumph of marketing as much as of morality. In 1804 Mrs Anne

Barbauld wrote of Pamela: 'We can only consider her as the conscious possessor of a treasure, which she is wisely resolved not to part with but for its just price.' It was precisely this market value of chastity which Richardson's subtitle, 'Virtue Rewarded', seemed to emphasize, as though holding out the prospect of material rewards for moral conduct. By concentrating instead on male chastity, Fielding may be seen as attempting to redefine the concept of virginity as a Christian ideal rather than a social asset. In essence he presents it as an ideal which prohibits an individual from entering into deceitful or exploitative relationships. At one point Adams declares that he cannot recall ever having told a lie (II, 3). At least, he adds when challenged, 'never a malicious one, I am certain ... nor with a design to injure the reputation of any man living'. Joseph's chastity is a virtue of the same kind. It represents a refusal to lie (no pun intended) with his body. What Fielding wishes to emphasize is not bodily virginity as a kind of selfish, quasi-materialistic hoarding instinct, but rather a form of active chastity which embodies a moral commitment to truth and fidelity. He also makes strenuous efforts to assure us that Joseph's chastity is by no means incompatible with a passionate vitality and healthy natural instincts. Yet, for all that, it cannot be said that Fielding's attitudes to this subject are entirely clear or consistent. As Brissenden writes: 'He never fully resolved the contradictions involved in attempting to reconcile his Christian idealism and his sense of sexual honesty.' In *Joseph Andrews* his most satisfactory attempts to reconcile these two elements are contained in his pictures of wedded love. Fielding offers us three images of happy marriages, all of them demonstrating certain key ingredients. Wilson is never happier than when playing with his children or sharing simple domestic pleasures with his wife. 'You cannot conceive the delight I have in my little ones. Would you not despise me, if you saw me stretched on the ground, and my children playing round me' (III, 4). On the contrary, Adams replies, 'I should reverence the sight.' Though kept apart from wife and family for much of the book, Adams's celebration of the role of paterfamilias is a further confirmation of the importance of the domestic life. His own marriage is not exactly idealized, though. Our first introduction to his domestic situation is with this phrase: 'The parson and his wife had just ended a long dispute when the lovers came to the door' (IV, 8). Mrs Adams has a habit of chiding and contradicting her husband for his unworldly ways, while Adams himself has a tendency to act the pedagogue with his children, combining the roles of proud father and anxious schoolmaster. The result is a kind of comic mayhem and disputations which, though sometimes warm, are never ill natured. Finally, we are informed in the last chapter that Fanny is 'not at present very able to bustle much' in her dairy, being 'extremely big with her first child'. In his pictures of all three marriages Fielding links love with its natural consequence in fecundity. These are no town gallantries or lecherous intrigues, but healthy natural appetites leading to happy family lives. It is typical of the slight touches by which he suggests a sense of fulfilment that Fanny should not just be big, but *extremely* big with her first child. Plumpness and ripeness have always been essential elements in her attractiveness, suggesting a natural appetite and healthy capacity for life. Here she moves directly from shy maiden to young mother, and her sensuality is safely and organically linked to her natural role.

This endorsement of the importance of sexual love in marriage is further confirmed by some ironic comedy at Adams's expense when he seeks to counsel Joseph on marital behaviour. The whole episode is nicely shaped as a comic set-piece, combining a theatrical sense of timing with a satirist's eye for allusive detail. Joseph, fearful of Lady Booby's designs to prevent his marriage with Fanny, urges Adams to perform the ceremony immediately by special licence. This plea provokes Adams to some of his most comically sententious utterances.

'Joseph,' says he, 'I wish this haste doth not arise rather from your impatience than your fear: but as it certainly springs from one of these causes, I will examine both. Of each of these therefore in their turn; and first, for the first of these, namely, impatience. Now, child, I must inform you, that if in your purposed marriage with this young woman, you have no intention but the indulgence of carnal appetites, you are guilty of a very heinous sin. Marriage was ordained for nobler purposes, as you will learn when you hear the service provided on that occasion read to you. Nay perhaps, if you are a good lad, I shall give you a sermon *gratis*, wherein I shall demonstrate how little regard ought to be had to the flesh on such occasions. The text will be, child, Matthew the 5th, and part of the 28th verse, *Whosoever looketh on a woman so as to lust after her*. The latter part I shall omit, as foreign to my purpose. Indeed all such brutal lusts and affections are to be greatly subdued, if not totally eradicated, before the vessel can be said to be consecrated to honour. To marry with a view of gratifying those inclinations is a prostitution of that holy ceremony, and must entail a curse on all who so lightly undertake it. If, therefore, this haste arises from impatience, you are to correct, and not give way to it. Now as to the second head which I proposed to speak to . . .' (IV, 8)

Note how Adams delivers his remarks according to a formal rhetorical pattern of heads and divisions. This pompous, analytical arrangement is a sure sign that his sentiments are to be taken with more than a pinch of scepticism, since Adams's normal – and more reliable – reactions to his young friend's fears are spontaneous and instinctive, not measured and

81

academic. We are presented with an immediate comic contrast between Joseph's desperation and Adams's formality. The language too shifts from its usual homely style into sermonizing formulas. This is Adams on his hobby-horse, and Fielding pokes gentle fun at him. The mockery is maintained in the text which Adams selects, since the latter part of the verse which he omits as 'foreign' to his purpose concerns adultery. The verse, in fact, reads: 'But I say unto you, That whoever looketh on a woman to lust after her hath committed adultery with her already in his heart,' which is hardly a caution appropriate for a wedding.

Adams continues in this same sententious vein until Fielding introduces the neat volte-face effect already noted. Adams sagely opines that 'no Christian ought so to set his heart on any person or thing in this world, but that whenever it shall be required or taken from him in any manner by divine Providence, he may be able, peaceably, quietly, and contentedly to resign it'. At that very moment he receives word that his youngest son has drowned. It was one of the tests of the original Abraham that he should be willing to sacrifice his son to his faith, but this modern Abraham shows an entirely human inability to resign himself as peaceably, quietly and contentedly as he recommended to the vicissitudes of fate. And it is a sure sign that Fielding recognizes family love as a support, not a threat, to true Christianity that he immediately introduces the lost little boy, bedraggled but safe. Adams's reaction is just what we would expect. He 'kissed and embraced his son a thousand times, and danced about the room like one frantick'. This instinctive physical response is in direct contrast with his cold formulaic precepts to Joseph. Yet Fielding carries this comic situation one step further by showing that Adams has actually learnt nothing from these experiences. No sooner has he recovered from his emotions than he resumes the same sententious theme.

> When these tumults were over, the parson taking Joseph aside, proceeded thus – 'No Joseph, do not give too much way to thy passions, if thou dost expect happiness.' – The patience of Joseph, nor perhaps of Job, could bear no longer; he interrupted the parson, saying, 'it was easier to give advice than take it, nor did he perceive he could so entirely conquer himself . . .'

This consistent gap between what Adams says and how he reacts is an essential part of his comic charm. His generous instincts continually get the better of his stoical resolutions, revealing him as both benign and eccentric, a kind of saintly innocent. The set-piece concludes with a smart piece of domestic comedy, with his wife having the last word. When Joseph declares that he fears he may be guilty of some sin, for 'I shall love without any moderation, I am sure,' Adams retorts, 'You talk foolishly and childishly.' This is the opportunity for his wife to intervene and contradict him, saying, 'you talk more foolishly yourself'. Indeed, Adams is a holy fool with a childlike lack of worldly skills. It is left to his wife to assure us: 'I am certain you do not preach as you practise,' though, in fact, we hardly need such assurance. The whole atmosphere of the parson's life convinces us that he combines spiritual and human love in his treatment of all his fellow creatures. It is Mrs Adams who firmly concludes this little debate, telling Joseph quite simply to 'love your wife with all your body and your soul too'. Fielding's resolution of the conflict between Christianity and sexuality is contained in this clear and natural endorsement of marriage.

Social Satire

Apart from these central moral preoccupations, we find a good deal of incidental social satire throughout the novel. In particular Fielding offers a number of ironic insights into two worlds that he knew well: the law courts and the playhouses. Lawyers, magistrates and constables appear throughout this, as through many of Fielding's other works. There is the lawyer in the stagecoach during the 'Good Samaritan' episode (I, 12) who plays the part of the learned Pharisee, full of legal precedents but oblivious to moral responsibilities. There is Tom Suckbribe the constable (I, 16) who conveniently allows the thief to escape. There is the lawyer who fans the dispute between Adams and Tow-wouse, hoping to persuade either or both of them to engage in a costly legal suit for damages (II, 5). There is the ignorant, drunken, fox-hunting magistrate who treats the law as a kind of superior blood sport, but who instantly acquits Adams as soon as he is assured he is a gentleman and not a vagabond (II, 11). There is Lawyer Scout who dispenses a special brand of Scout's law, which is merely the gratification through legal jargon of whatever the whims or desires of the local patron or landowner – in this case Lady Booby – may be. However, in this instance Fielding offers a partial defence of the legal profession from association with the likes of Scout. He tells us explicitly that Scout 'was one of those fellows, who without any knowledge of the law, or being bred to it, take upon them, in defiance of an act of parliament, to act as lawyers in the country, and are called so. They are the pests of society, and a scandal to a profession, to which indeed they do not belong' (IV, 3). In other words Fielding wishes to expose those charlatans whose ignorance and self-seeking bring the law into disrepute, rather than to attack the law itself. But on at least a few occasions there are ironic asides which convince us that Fielding was unhappy at the severity of the law's penalties for some offences. First, the postillion who acts the part of the Good Samaritan to Joseph, stripping off his great coat, 'his only garment', to cover Joseph's nakedness, was subsequently transported, we are told, 'for robbing a hen-roost' (I, 12). Secondly, there is Lawyer Scout's illiterate, trumped-up charge against Fanny and Joseph, which alleges

Joseph Andrews with a nife cut one hassel-twig, of the value, as he believes, of 3 half pence, or thereabouts; and he saith, that the said Francis Goodwill was likewise walking on the grass out of the said path in the said felde, and did receive and karry in her hand the said twig, and so was cumfarting, eading and abatting to the said Joseph therein ... (IV, 5)

When Squire Booby protests at the idea of committing two people to the Bridewell (prison) for the sake of a twig, Lawyer Scout merely boasts of his own magnanimity. 'Yes,' said the lawyer, 'and with great lenity too; for if we had called it a young tree they would have been both hanged.' This may strike modern readers as a grotesque piece of satiric exaggeration, but it does, in fact, accurately indicate the savagery of English law, particularly regarding the theft or damage of property, in the period. Pat Rogers gives a chilling summary of eighteenth-century legal penalties at the start of *The Augustan Vision*:

Hanging crimes ranged from murder, rape, sodomy, arson and forgery through burglary, house-breaking, maiming cattle and shooting at a revenue officer to cutting down trees in an avenue, concealing the death of a bastard child, destroying turnpikes and sending threatening letters. Lesser punishments, headed by transportation, were reserved for such comparatively venial offences as petty larcenies of a shilling or less, ripping lead, and bigamy. Coiners might still be burnt at Tyburn; merely to be present at a riot and shout encouragement was a capital felony. (*The Augustan Vision*, pp. 7–8)

In both these instances it is clear that the penalties of the law are totally out of keeping with the moral characters of the individuals charged, which demonstrates the law's emphasis on social conformity rather than moral integrity. It is this which makes it a familiar target for Fielding's satire.

Like the theatre the law serves as both a subject and a metaphor throughout the novel. Sometimes he uses it as the basis for an extended simile. Thus, when offering a mock-heroic image of Slipslop's emotional perplexity, torn between Honour and Pride, Pity and Revenge, in her feelings for Joseph, Fielding introduces this decorative analogy:

So have I seen, in the Hall of Westminster; where Serjeant Bramble hath been retained on the right side, and Serjeant Puzzle on the left; the balance of opinion (so equal were their fees) alternatively incline to either scale. Now Bramble throws in an argument, and Puzzle's scale strikes the beam; again, Bramble shares the like fate, overpowered by the weight of Puzzle. Here Bramble hits, there Puzzle strikes; here one has you, there t'other has you; 'till at last all becomes one scene of confusion in the tortured minds of the hearers; equal wagers are laid on the success, and neither judge nor jury can possibly make any thing of the matter; all things are so enveloped by the careful serjeants in doubt and obscurity. (I, 9)

There is a deliberate quality of self-indulgence about this leisurely simile which demonstrates Fielding's delight in playing with both his characters and his readers. As he remarks at the end of the chapter, 'If it was only our present business to make similes, we could produce many more to this purpose.' By such means he reminds us that all the elements in this novel – plot, characters, imagery and asides – are at his disposal to manipulate at will. This image of legal disputation as an arbitrary see-saw is an ironic comment not only on the volatile emotions warring in Slipslop's breast, but on the autocratic power of the novelist to arrange all the careful antitheses between art and nature, hypocrisy and innocence, to produce his chosen result.

Elsewhere in the novel he has great fun ridiculing legalistic jargon and casuistry but often the pattern of argument and debate suggests the adversarial structure of legal proceedings. In all these ways the atmosphere of the law court permeates the book, and enforces a permanent sense of judgement and arbitrament. Usually the terms of that judgement are concerned with the balance, or conflict, between social and moral values, as we are required to contrast the standards of the world with the ideals of Christianity. But if we are the jury in this court, Fielding's irony ensures that we are well vetted, and retains full control of both the evidence and the sentence.

However, if Fielding's novel is partly a court of justice, it is also in part a theatre. Theatrical similes abound. In order to impress upon us the sudden pallor in Lady Booby's face at Joseph's mention of his virtue, Fielding offers this analogy:

You have seen the faces, in the eighteen-penny gallery, when through the trap-door, to soft or no musick, Mr Bridgewater, Mr William Mills, or some other of ghostly appearance, hath ascended with a face all pale with powder, and a shirt all bloody with ribbons. (I, 8)

Bridgewater and Mills were actors who often appeared in Fielding's own comedies, but who also played Shakespearean tragedy. Fielding also makes reference to the great theatrical impresario John Rich, whose repertoire of pantomimes and harlequinades introduced a variety of new stage effects. The traumatic effects of love on Lady Booby's mind are compared to some of Rich's most surreal *coups de théâtre*: 'Not the great Rich, who turns men into monkeys, wheelbarrows, and whatever else best humours his fancy, hath so strangely metamorphosed the human shape' (I, 7). Fielding exploits theatrical devices and effects, such as the soliloquy of Lady Booby (I, 8); he employs dramatic ironies, such as when the man of courage is revealed as a coward (II, 9), or when Adams's stoical theories are undermined by personal tragedy (IV, 8). In his comments on plays and players, as in his remarks on the law and lawyers, Fielding seeks to defend the profession against charlatans and buffoons. The set-piece debate between the poet and the player (III, 10), which is described as being 'of no other Use in this History, but to divert the Reader', is an example of theatrical gossip much in the manner of the first act of Sheridan's *The Critic*. On the whole, the modern reader is frankly little concerned whether Fielding's disparagement of such obscure plays as Frowd's *Phelotas* or Mallet's *Eurydice* is meant to be ironic or otherwise. One may suspect that Fielding had a certain sympathy with the poet's observation that 'the reason you have no good new plays is evident, it is from your discouragement of authors' (III, 10). Yet one should not forget that the poet and player of this set-piece are among the 'ridiculous, odious and absurd' companions of the 'roasting' squire. The poet composes some doggerel verses ridiculing Adams, of which the parson is content to say merely that he would rather be the subject than the composer of such malicious sentiments. The player repeats a number of attacks on the clergy drawn from plays, which elicit this pained rebuke from Adams: 'I am sure such plays are a scandal to the government which permits them' (III, 7), a sentiment perhaps somewhat surprising to find in the work of an author whose career as a playwright had been curtailed by government censorship. Adams is consistently suspicious of plays and players. When told that a play may sell for a hundred guineas, while a collection of sermons may not fetch twelve pence (I, 16–17), Adams protests: 'But is there no difference between conveying good or ill instructions to mankind?' (I, 17). The bookseller's reply, that Walpole's Licensing Act may shortly 'bring them both to the same footing', that is, make both equally unsaleable, is not at all the kind of reassurance that Adams requires. For Mr Wilson a period first as a play-goer, and then as a would-be playwright, are inevitable steps on the downward path of the 'rake's progress'. Playwriting comes after free-thinking but before gambling on the route to destruction. Wilson describes in detail the miserable condition of the hack writer, a plight depicted at length in Fielding's earlier comic play *The Author's Farce*:

I now experienced what is worse than poverty, or rather what is the worst consequence of poverty, I mean attendance and dependance on the great. Many a morning have I waited hours in the cold parlours of men of quality, where after seeing the lowest rascals in lace and embroidery, the pimps and buffoons in fashion admitted, I have been somtimes told on sending in my name, that my lord could not possibly see me this morning: a sufficient assurance that I should never more get entrance into that house. Sometimes I have been at last admitted, and the great men hath thought proper to excuse himself, by telling me he was tied up. '*Tied up*,' says Adams, 'pray what's that?' (III, 3)

In Wilson's explanation of this phrase, Fielding reveals his own dislike of the haphazard and humiliating processes of literary patronage, and in particular attacks the system of publication 'by subscription' which had recently degenerated into a mercenary racket. Subscription publication had begun to flourish at the beginning of the eighteenth century. It was a system whereby a publisher would seek to attract advanced orders for a prestigious work from a number of wealthy and distinguished patrons, in return guaranteeing to print their names in his grandest type at the front of the book. Instead of a single patron being required to support a struggling author, a group of patrons, for a relatively modest sum, could find themselves honoured in print as members of an enlightened club of literary *cognoscenti*. Some authors, as Fielding notes, did particularly well out of this system. Jacob Tonson's subscription edition of *Poems on Several Occasions* by Matthew Prior (1719) earned its author 'some four thousand guineas', while Bernard Lintot's subscription edition of Pope's translation of Homer yielded Pope about £9,000. Yet, as the vogue for this kind of publication developed, less scrupulous publishers and less diligent authors saw it as a means of making easy money and, as Wilson notes, subscriptions were solicited for 'what was not writ, nor ever intended'. By this means, the device of subscription publishing became a kind of confidence trick or 'a tax upon the public'.

Wilson soon descends still further from would-be playwright to a hack scrivener for lawyers, yet here too his artistic ambitions are merely the occasion for ridicule. One lawyer acquaintance laughs at him, saying, 'he was afraid I should turn his deeds into plays'. In the Temple and at the coffee-houses, Wilson encounters the same contempt:

> Not to tire you with instances of this kind from others, I found that Plato himself did not hold poets in greater abhorrence than these men of business do. Whenever I durst venture to a coffee-house, which was on Sundays only, a whisper ran round the room, which was constantly attended with a sneer – *That's poet Wilson ...* (III, 3)

Sundays were always the bankrupt's day of freedom, since one could not be arrested for debt on the sabbath. Plato wished to exclude poets from his ideal republic on account of their allegedly corrupting influence, a judgement which has been used to dignify the prejudices of philistines ever since. Obviously much of Wilson's narrative at this point has the authentic ring of remembered experiences, since Fielding too had for many years hovered between the law courts and the theatre. Luckily for him, though, most of the desperation is imagined, not remembered, for his own early success had been rapid and assured.

Adams is more tolerant than Plato, and actually quotes from Addison's *Cato* at one point (III, 5), which is, he says, 'the only English tragedy I ever read'. Elsewhere he says, 'I never heard of any plays for a Christian to read, but *Cato* and *The Conscious Lovers* and I must own in the latter there are things almost solemn enough for a sermon' (III, 11). *The Conscious Lovers* by Richard Steele (1722) is the kind of sentimental comedy, with a strong moralizing attack on vice and an endorsement of marriage, of which Adams might well be expected to approve. These remarks of his are in response to Joseph's quotation of some lines from *Macbeth*, which Adams reproves as 'heathenism'. Yet clearly we are expected to treat some of his attacks on the theatre as part of his innocent unworldliness, and as further indications of his sentimental and unsophisticated literary taste. However, we should never forget his abiding passion for Aeschylus, the most ancient of playwrights, and his learned appreciation of such heathenish poets as Homer and Virgil. Here again we have another example of the novel's dual tone. For undoubtedly there is an element of self-deprecating irony at work here, as Fielding deliberately uses the persona of Adams to adopt a pose of literary simplicity, and to poke fun at the kind of literary sophistication which bubbles through all his burlesque dramas and animates the digressions of the narrator.

As a satirist Fielding, like Hogarth, includes some caricatures of real people among his fictional creations. Peter Pounce is clearly intended to be a portrait of the notorious Peter Walter of Stalbridge, a man who, through assiduous meanness and sharp practice as a steward, had acquired a steady accumulation of wealth and landed property in Dorset, Somerset and Wiltshire. In the writings of Pope, Swift and Fielding, Walter is constantly presented as the supreme example of the 'dextrous attorney', equally adept at cheating landowners and exploiting tenants. Similarly Beau Didapper would have been recognizable to contemporary readers as Lord John Hervey of Ickworth, whose effeminate and epicene manner was famously attacked in Pope's portrait of the 'butterfly' Sporus.

> *this bug with gilded wings*
> *This painted child of dirt, that stinks and stings . . .*
> *Amphibious thing! that acting either part,*
> *The trifling head, or the corrupted heart,*
> *Fop at the toilet, flatt'rer at the board,*
> *Now trips a lady, and now struts a lord.*

(Epistle to Dr Arbuthnot, II, 309–10; 326–9)

In the same way, in the second painting of *The Rake's Progress* series, one can see Hogarth's fictional rake surrounded by some recognizable real-life figures from the 'polite' world of fashionable diversions. There is Charles Bridgeman, the celebrated landscape gardener, and Dubois, the well-known French duellist, who is observed with sulky condescension by James Figg, the English prize-fighter and broad-sword champion. Yet, in both cases, Fielding and Hogarth are careful to offer a universal image as well as this particular one, reminding us of the species that stands behind the individual. In Hogarth's case his cunning exploitation of physiognomy transforms the faces of his subjects into indictments of their morals. Similarly Fielding's description of the behaviour of Peter Pounce and Beau Didapper makes them not merely figures of personal caricature, but living examples of avarice and affectation respectively. Against these real-life caricatures he also sets some references to real-life heroes. In both *Joseph Andrews* and *Tom Jones* Ralph Allen of Prior Park near Bath is singled out for praise. Allen was a philanthropist, patron of the arts and founder of the British postal service. In *Tom Jones* Fielding used Allen as his model for Squire Allworthy and in *Joseph Andrews* he is the unnamed commoner 'raised higher above the multitude by superior talents, than is the power of his prince to exalt him' (III, 1). Fielding's use of such contemporary figures in his novel lends the satiric fiction an added air of authenticity. It also introduces a valuable element of social reality into the charming blend of art and nature, and suggests an interrelationship between literature and life. Adams and Allen are equally at home in the world of *Joseph Andrews*, which is as much a satiric portrait of England as a moral parable.

The Clergy

Clergymen, like lawyers, figure prominently throughout *Joseph Andrews*. In fact, in addition to Adams there are six other clergymen presented in the novel, all of them corrupt or incompetent to some degree, of whom Barnabas and Trulliber are the most memorable. It has even been plausibly argued that, in addition to his more general moral concerns, Fielding partly intended the novel as a defence of the lower clergy. In the *Champion* during the spring of 1740 Fielding included a series of four essays on the theme of 'An Apology for the Clergy' (using 'apology' in the traditional sense of 'defence' rather than as an expression of regret). Like Swift, Fielding was worried that a clergyman's gown was commonly treated as 'a general mark of contempt'. The lower clergy in particular were often treated with condescension because of their poverty and their dependence on the whims of lay patrons. Poverty, Fielding observed in *The Jacobite's Journal* (1748), 'brought more contempt on our own clergy, than hath been cast upon them by the utmost malice of infidels or libertines ... Not only the man of piety, but even he who professes a decent regard to religion, as to a wholesome civil institution, must agree in the necessity of preserving the priesthood from the contempt of the people.' The summary of Adams's own career (II, 8) is a satiric indictment of the temporal realities of an ecclesiastical system in which preferment was often in the gift of political patrons. 'I am an honest man, and would not do an ill thing to be made a bishop,' declares Adams. Such honesty is rewarded with the 'handsome income of twenty-three pounds a year', little enough when his livelihood is further 'circumscribed with a wife and six children' (I, 3). It should be noted that Adams, like Fielding, assumes that even in the Church, readiness to 'do an ill thing' is the surest route to the top. In its temporal, as opposed to its spiritual, role the Church is subject to the very same vanities and vices as any other institution of the state. In a sense, then, Adams's poverty, his tattered cassock and dishevelled wig are badges of his honesty. When at the end he, like Joseph and Fanny, is favoured by good fortune and Mr Booby offers him a second living of '£130 a year', he is instinctively suspicious. 'He at first refused it, resolving not to quit his parishioners, with whom he had lived so long' (IV, 16). This is a natural endorsement of his instinct throughout the novel to put pastoral convictions before worldly considerations. Only when he recollects that he will now be able to keep a curate to share his duties does Adams assent to accept the reward that awaits all 'good' characters at the end of Fielding's novels.

Yet if the poverty of clergymen, resulting from an unjust and corrupt system of patronage, was one reason for the contempt in which they were often held, other reasons were to be found in the conduct and demeanour of the clergy themselves. For, as Fielding wrote in the *Champion* (1740), 'as nothing can hurt religion so much as a contempt of the clergy, so nothing can justify, or indeed cause any such contempt but their own bad lives'.

As with the law and the stage, Fielding's main satiric purpose is to attack those whose behaviour brought the whole vocation into disrepute. There is Barnabas, vain, perfunctory in his duties, fonder of punch than of preaching, a man 'who loved sermons no better than a grocer doth figs'. It is characteristic, as Martin Battestin has remarked, that 'he vigorously denounces the only doctrine of Whitefield's preaching worth preserving (in the opinion of Adams and Fielding)'; namely, the idea that 'a clergyman ought to be always preaching and praying' (I, 17). He is particularly unhappy at Whitefield's recommendation of the ideal of Christian poverty; Whitefield 'would make mankind believe, that the poverty and low estate which was recommended to the church in its infancy, and was only temporary doctrine adapted to her under persecution, was to be preserved in her flourishing and established state' (I, 17). Then there is Trulliber, gross, avaricious and autocratic, a pig-farmer six days of the week and a parson only on Sundays. Trulliber, as we have seen, uses the doctrine of justification by faith as the perfect excuse for selfishness and hypocrisy. There is the avaricious parson in Adams's parish whose unavailing litigation concerning 'a *modus* ... of several shillings *per annum*' had so far achieved no greater success 'than the pleasure (which he used indeed frequently to say was no small one) of reflecting that he had utterly undone many of the poor tenants, though he had at the same time greatly impoverished himself' (I, 3). (A *modus* was the fixed monetary substitute for the value of the tithes of produce paid by parishioners to the church.)

There is the arrogant parson who 'instead of esteeming his poor parishioners as a part of his family, seems rather to consider them as not of the same species with himself' (II, 16), and who struts through the churchyard 'like a turkey-cock through rows of his parishioners; who bow to him with as much submission and are as unregarded as a set of servile courtiers by the proudest prince in Christendom'. There is the ignorant parson who declares that Adams's Aeschylus is 'a manuscript of one of the Fathers' (that is the leaders of the early Church), and is keen to sell it to a nobleman 'who would give a great deal of money for such a piece of antiquity' (II, 11). Ignorance here is, of course, linked to avarice, since this parson is interested in the financial, rather than the spiritual, value of a supposed piece of scripture. Finally there is the political parson who contrives to have Adams expelled from his living for failing to put politics before conscience (II, 8). These clergymen join Thwackum and Supple (*Tom Jones*) and a host of other vain, avaricious, corrupt, proud, time-serving, ignorant clergymen that abound in the pages of Fielding's writings. But set against all these is a figure like Adams who embodies all that is honest, truthful, faithful and charitable in the lower clergy. Adams's statements are clear and uncompromising declarations of his commitment to Christian ideals: 'Out of love to yourself,' he insists, 'you should confine yourself to truth' (II, 3); 'I am an honest man and would not do an ill thing to be made a bishop' (II, 8). His vehement reaction that the life of the fashionable man-about-town, as described by Wilson, 'is below the life of an animal' is an instinctive assertion of the moral values and integrity which are inseparable from his notion of humanity. Yet, more important than all these statements is the way that Adams *acts*. 'By their fruits you shall know them' (Matthew 7:16) is an aphorism cherished equally by Adams and Fielding. Adams's acts are the living model of Christian benevolence and charity. The reception which he receives from his parishioners is the fitting testimonial to his life of idealism in action: 'They flocked about him like dutiful children round an indulgent parent, and vied with each other in demonstrations of duty and love' (IV, 1).

Fielding's Language

'Several words, in all languages,' Fielding observed in the *Champion* in January 1740, 'have with great injustice been wrested and perverted ... and, by long use and corruption, been brought to convey ideas foreign to their original signification.' As a satirist Fielding was consistently exercised by the abuses of language – in particular by that form of sophisticated euphemism by which abstract moral terms such as virtue, honour, chastity or prudence were perverted to disguise and justify self-interest. His theories of language were mainly derived from John Locke's *Essay Concerning Human Understanding* (1690), in which Locke expressed his own anxieties about the malleability of moral terms:

> When we speak of *justice* or *gratitude* we frame to ourselves no imagination of anything existing, which we would conceive, but our thoughts terminate in the abstract idea of those virtues, and look no further. (*Essay*, III, 5)

In another *Champion* article (November 1739) Fielding made a similar point: 'What we look on as power, honour, wisdom, piety etc. ... are often not the things themselves, but the appearances only.' Such a remark, however, does convey the optimistic implication that the 'things themselves' could and did have a real existence independent of language, though often obscured by ignorant or corrupt usage. Locke, who described language as 'the great conduit' of human knowledge, designated a number of prevalent abuses of language which could poison or corrupt the linguistic currency of society. Chief and most common of these was simple ignorance or carelessness, whereby the sounds of particular words were used without any clear or distinct ideas attached to them. This is the kind of abuse that Fielding satirizes in the character of Slipslop, 'a mighty affecter of hard words' (I, 3), who uses words rather like random missiles, paying more attention to their sonority and weight than to their specific meanings. In this respect she may be seen as a prototype for the famous Mrs Malaprop in Sheridan's *The Rivals*. Another abuse mentioned by Locke is an 'affected obscurity', and Fielding is merciless in his ridicule of the opaque professional jargon by which lawyers and doctors seek to bamboozle the public. But perhaps most significant of all in Locke's view were those 'wilful faults and neglects' by which men used language to disguise rather than express their purposes. 'I may have the idea of virtues or vices; and names also, but apply them amiss: e.g. when I apply the name frugality to that idea which others call and signify by this sound, covetousness' (*Essay*, III, 10). It is indeed on this form of abuse, the casuistical manipulation of virtuous terms to disguise vicious purposes, that Fielding concentrates his satire.

Some years later in the *Covent-Garden Journal* (1752) Fielding published an ironic 'Modern Glossary' in which he offered a satiric reinterpretation or decoding of a number of abstract terms in current use in fashionable society. His technique in this glossary might be compared with a modern satirist revealing the reality behind the deceptive hyperbole of public relations prose, or reminding us that an estate agent's description of a 'compact investment opportunity' really refers to a tiny ruin. Thus in Fielding's 'Modern Glossary' the term 'gallantry' is decoded to mean 'fornication and adultery'; 'honour' is reduced to mere duelling; 'temperance' becomes 'want of spirit'; and 'virtue' and 'vice' are dismissed as mere 'subjects of discourse', that is, conventional tropes for parlour games or academic debates. They are things to talk about, but never to take seriously. Throughout his career Fielding was concerned by this process of linguistic devaluation by which moral absolutes were converted into social accessories. Lord Chesterfield once remarked that fashionable ladies would 'take a word and change it, like guineas into shillings for pocket money, to be employed on the several occasional purposes of the day'. In the *Champion* (August 1740) Fielding composed a satiric essay which reveals the same inventive wit that animates the linguistic concerns in *Joseph Andrews* and *Tom Jones*. Mr Job Vinegar describes a custom which prevails among the people of the imaginary land of Pteghsiumgski, called 'GD BRDNG, a phrase not to be translated in English by any other (how coarse soever it may seem) than *lying*'. Notice how Fielding mimics the sound of the fashionable aristocratic drawl by omitting the vowels in 'good breeding'. By this means he also simultaneously suggests that their understanding of the word is as corrupt as their pronunciation. In the same way, in *Shamela* the heroine's references to her 'vartue' indicate the gap between the original moral value and its social counterfeit. In *Joseph Andrews* we are frequently reminded how good humour and good breeding are frequently mistaken for good nature, though, for all their resemblances, they remain as distinct as frugality and covetousness. 'Men are chiefly betrayed,' Fielding observes in his 'Essay on the Knowledge of the Characters of Men', 'by a gross but common mistake of good-humour for good-nature. Two qualities so far from bearing any resemblance to each other, that they are almost opposites.'

In other *Champion* papers Fielding attacked the jargon of the professions and accused Colley Cibber of murdering the English language – all of which goes to prove that for him the issue of linguistic corruption was no mere piece of cranky fastidiousness, but a serious moral concern affecting the health of society.

In *Joseph Andrews* Slipslop is the first abuser of language that we meet, but initially her 'hard words' seem merely an innocent form of ignorant affectation. Her comic neologisms result in some ludicrous verbal incongruities, such as when she tells Lady Booby that Joseph is 'horribly *indicted* to wenching' and is a 'strong healthy *luscious* boy' (I, 7). Her elaborate linguistic pretensions make a nice contrast with Lady Booby's condescending aristocratic slang and terseness. She 'never spoke of any of her country neighbours by any other appellation than that of the *brutes*', and calls Pamela 'a little vixen' (I, 8). Slipslop's language is an indication of her social pretensions, just as Lady Booby's vulgarisms show the lowness of mind that condescends to an infatuation with a footman. Particularly characteristic of Lady Booby's verbal style is a form of rhetorical repetition that owes much to theatrical comedy. When Joseph protests his virtue (I, 8), she runs through an arpeggio of the emotions as she dissects the term:

> 'Your virtue! (said the lady recovering after a silence of two minutes) I shall never survive it. Your virtue! Intolerable confidence! Have you the assurance to pretend, that when a lady demeans herself to throw aside the rules of decency, in order to honour you with the highest favour in her power, your virtue should resist her inclination? That when she had conquer'd her own virtue, she should find an obstruction in yours?' (I, 8)

She actually repeats the word 'virtue' six times in this paragraph. Even more devastating to her pride is Parson Adams's innocent praise of Fanny's beauty when he calls her 'the handsomest woman, gentle or simple, that ever appeared in the parish'. Lady Booby explodes with jealousy at this:

> '... Ridiculous! Beauty indeed, – a country wench a beauty. – I shall be sick whenever I hear beauty mentioned again. – And so this wench is to stock the parish with beauties, I hope ...' (IV, 2)

Like a twitching nerve, Lady Booby's injured vanity flicks out ten repetitions of the word 'beauty', by which time she has virtually twisted the word into the epitome of all the vices.

Similar to Slipslop's linguistic aberrations are the verbal errors of the bullying captain who assists at the 'roasting' of Parson Adams. When Adams wishes that his tormentors might have 'a little more sense, as well as humanity', the captain responds.

The captain answer'd with a surly look and accent, 'that he hoped he did not mean to reflect on him; d—n him, he had as much imanity as another, and if any man said he had not, he would convince him of his mistake by cutting his throat.' Adams smiling, said, 'he believed he had spoke right by accident.' (III, 7)

Here the captain's snarl of 'imanity' bears about as close a resemblance to the word 'humanity' as his bullying manner does to the concept itself.

The linguistic corruptions of the lawyers and doctors are less harmless than Slipslop's morphological snobbery. She, at least, is a corrupter of language through ignorance, whereas their jargon is specifically designed to assist them to conceal predatory instincts under remedial pretensions. The Pharisaical lawyer in the coach who encounters the naked Joseph lying in a ditch makes some 'pretty jests' on his condition, using a string of legal terms to convey a series of crude *double entendres* on his wretched state:

He said, 'if Joseph and the lady were alone, he would be the more capable of making a *conveyance* to her, as his *affairs* were not *fettered* with any *incumbrance*; he'd warrant, he soon suffered a *recovery* by a writ of *entry*, which was the proper way to create *heirs in tail*; that for his own part, he would engage to make so *firm a settlement* in a coach, that there should be no danger of an *ejectment* . . .' (I, 12)

The ignorant magistrate (II, 11) uses a bluster of Latin terms to cover up his total lack of understanding of the laws he administers; while the doctor (I, 14) uses a gibberish of Greek and Latin tags and polysyllabic jargon to increase his reputation and his fee. Yet Joseph's recovery, as we have noted, owes more to either the rabbit or the fowl that he consumes (the narrator is uncertain which) than to the doctor's much vaunted *sanative soporiferous* draughts which remain 'untouched in the window' (I, 16).

The proper end of language, in Locke's view, was so that a man 'may make known his ideas to the hearer'. But Bernard Mandeville, author of the notorious satiric poem *The Fable of the Bees*, took a more cynical view. 'The first design of speech,' he wrote, 'was to persuade others either to give credit to what the speaking person would have them believe; or else to act or suffer such things, as he would compel them to act or suffer if they were entirely in his power.' For Mandeville, then, the prime function of language was not the understanding of ideas, but the exercise of power. The professions, as Fielding shows them, too often use a bewildering jargon precisely to increase their power by limiting the layman's understanding of their terms.

Another fashionable method of torturing, if not murdering, the English language which Fielding deplored was the affectation for decorating and interlarding straightforward English phrases with an ornamentation of foreign words. Bellarmine is addicted to this affectation (II, 4), as is the traveller who begs Miss Grave-airs not to be frightened at the fight between Adams and Tow-wouse which leaves Adams all covered in hog's-blood, 'for here had been only a little boxing, which he said to their *disgracia* the English were *accustomata* to' (II, 5). Beau Didapper's conversation, though English in terms of vocabulary, has all the tortured affectations which, Fielding assures us in a footnote, 'is taken verbatim from very polite conversation'. In writing this he may seek to remind us of Swift's volume of *Polite Conversation* (1738), which transforms a catalogue of clichés into an absurd comedy of manners. Plain and simple language, like plain and simple food, is what Fielding professes to value: an honest and natural diet and dialect, without affectations or pretensions in either. However, he does make a small exception in favour of Adams's habit of quoting classical phrases. This is another of those innocent vanities, like Adams's pedantic and stoic assertions, which show that he too has some normal human frailties. But his deep knowledge of classical literature also indicates his recognition of wider human sympathies, embracing not only the 'extended family' of his parish, but also taking account of the achievements of humanity through the ages.

Perhaps the best illustration of the satiric antithesis between the moral and social 'meanings' of a word can be seen in the various uses of the word 'betters'. In an article in the *Covent-Garden Journal* Fielding wrote:

Of all the oppressions which the rich are guilty of, there seems to be none more impudent and unjust than their endeavour to rob the poor of a title which is most clearly the property of the latter. Not content with all the Honourables, Worshipfuls, Reverends, and a thousand other proud epithets which they exact of the poor, and for which they give in return nothing but dirt, scrub, mob, and such like, they have laid violent hands on a word, to which they have not the least pretence or shadow of any title. The word I mean is the comparative of the adjective good, namely BETTER, or as it is usually expressed in the plural number, BETTERS. An appellative which all the rich usurp to themselves and most shamefully use when they speak of, or to the poor: For do we not every day hear such phrases as these. *Do not be saucy to your BETTERS. Learn to behave yourself before your BETTERS. Pray know your BETTERS,* etc. It is possible that the rich have been so long in possession of this, that they now lay a kind of prescriptive claim to the property; but however that be, I doubt not but to make it appear, that if the word *Better* is to be understood as the comparative of *Good*, and is meant to convey an idea of superior goodness, it is with the highest impropriety applied to the rich, in comparison with the poor.

It is a mark of Joseph's innocence and humility that he should not question the identification of moral superiority with social status implicit in the word. He told Adams that

'he was perfectly content with the state to which he was called, that he should endeavour to improve his talent, which was all required of him, but not repine at his own lot, nor envy those of his betters.' (I, 3)

Slipslop, however, is more combative, and her comic-pathetic oxymoron 'my be-betters are wo-worse than me' (I, 17) catches the ironic ambiguity of the word nicely. Later she and Miss Grave-airs cross swords in what is more simply a question of snobbish point-scoring. Miss Grave-airs observes that she is not much used to stage-coaches.

'That may be, madam,' replied Slipslop, 'very good people do, and some people's betters, for aught I know.' Miss Grave-airs said, 'some folks might sometimes give their tongues a liberty, to some people that were their betters which did not become them: for her part, she was not used to converse with servants.' Slipslop returned, 'some people kept no servants to converse with ...' Miss Grave-airs cry'd, 'she believed her mistress would not encourage such sauciness to her betters.' 'My betters,' says Slipslop, 'who is my betters, pray?' 'I am your betters,' answered Miss Grave-airs, 'and I'll acquaint your mistress.' – At which Mrs Slipslop laughed aloud ... (II, 5)

The ironic effect is reinforced when Slipslop naïvely repeats the phrase as a social cliché, assuring Lady Booby that, far from being jealous of Joseph's supposed affairs with the wenches, she looked upon herself as his 'betters'. And when Adams cries out, snapping his fingers, that he wished all Fanny's 'betters were as good', he underlines the paradoxical contrast between the moral and social meanings of the word. Finally, when in her desperate attempt to reingratiate herself with Lady Booby, Slipslop returns to the word, the point is fully confirmed.

Slipslop then fell on Fanny, whom she hack'd and hew'd in the like barbarous manner, concluding with an observation that there was always something in those low-life creatures which must eternally distinguish them from their betters. (IV, 6)

In fact, what distinguishes such 'low-life creatures' as Fanny from their 'betters' like Lady Booby is an innocence which contains more natural nobility, gentility and honour than all their stylish clothes and titles, their etiquette and affected speech. Like the word 'virtue', or the word 'greatness' in *Jonathan Wild*, Fielding turns this social cliché on its head until the 'betters' are indeed worse. It is a thoroughly Christian form of paradox, putting down the mighty and raising the meek and humble.

Fielding's own language throughout the novel is the perfect embodiment of the linguistic values and virtues which he recommends. It combines the ironic detail and syntactical precision of a satirist steeped in classical forms with the freedom and energy of a more expansive and exuberant narrative style. Take, for example, this paragraph which describes the emotions of Mr Tow-wouse.

Mr Tow-wouse had for some time cast the languishing eyes of affection on this young maiden. He had laid hold on every opportunity of saying tender things to her, squeezing her by the hand, and sometimes of kissing her lips: for as the violence of his passion had considerably abated to Mrs Tow-wouse; so like water, which is stopt from its usual current in one place, it naturally sought a vent in another. Mrs Tow-wouse is thought to have perceived this abatement, and probably it added very little to the natural sweetness of her temper: for tho' she was as true to her husband as the dial to the sun, she was rather more desirous of being shone on, as being more capable of feeling his warmth. (I, 18)

Here, through the comic deployment of natural imagery, Fielding contrives simultaneously to excuse and ridicule Tow-wouse's adulterous desires. The opening sentence, with its deliberately hackneyed phrases 'languishing eyes' and 'young maiden' (when we know that Betty is so far from being a maiden that she required the attentions of the surgeon to cure her venereal infection), introduces a mock-romantic note. This is the language of courtly love made comic through the inappropriateness of the context. Yet Tow-wouse's desires are not simply those of a latter-day hero; they also have the inevitability of a force of nature such as water, which, being 'stopt from its usual current in one place, it naturally sought a vent in another'. Here too the ironic tone both dignifies and debases the emotion it describes. To compare love to a natural element might make it seem irresistible and noble, part of the natural order of things. Yet the exact phrasing here also suggests random promiscuity, like water seeping out wherever it can. The word 'vent' in particular is hardly a dignified term to describe the object of his affections, and reduces the whole emotion to a form of crude physical relief. And when in the following metaphor Mr Tow-wouse is compared with the sun, the same sense of mock-epic comedy surrounds the elemental image. For the humorous conceit which turns his wife into a human sun-dial suggests firstly the formality and passivity of her sexuality, only to hint at the frustrations that result from the 'abatement' of his feelings. In both images there is an ironic discrepancy between the elemental Mr Tow-wouse, who is first water and then sunshine, and the functional females who serve him as a 'vent' or a 'dial'. The overall effect is to make Tow-wouse himself ridiculous, and his desires a sad example of *folie de grandeur*. This paragraph, in fact, is the perfect preparation for the farcical scene in which he and Betty are caught *in flagrante delicto* on the following page.

I have described this short passage in some detail not because it is especially subtle or brilliant, but because it is typical of Fielding's narrative style. The language is simple but carefully considered; the tone is ironic but genial; the effect is an affirmation of humanity through the language of comedy.

The Reputation of *Joseph Andrews*

There is a traditional story that Fielding was amazed when the bookseller Millar offered him £200 for the manuscript of *Joseph Andrews*, together with some short pieces. Whatever his own view of the book, its reputation both at the time and since has been somewhat mixed. When it first appeared, the poet William Shenstone declared it 'a very mean performance ... the greater part is unnatural and unhumorous'. He considered Parson Adams 'tedious'. A French critic was equally damning and declared that 'dull burlesque is still more unsupportable than dull morality'. Arthur Murphy, writing in 1762, was of quite another opinion:

> The truth is, Fielding in this performance was employed in the very province for which his talents were peculiarly and happily formed; namely, the fabulous narration of some imagined action, which did occur, or might probably have occurred in human life. Nothing could be more happily conceived than the character of Parson Adams for the principal personage of the work; the humanity, and benevolence of affection, the goodness of heart, and the zeal for virtue, which come from him upon all occasions, attach us to Mr Adams in the most endearing manner.

For Sir John Hawkins, however, this goodness of heart was mere cant. In 1787 he wrote of Fielding:

> He was the inventor of that cant-phrase, goodness of heart, which is every day used as a substitute for probity, and means little more than the virtue of a horse or a dog; in short, he has done more towards corrupting the rising generation than any writer we know of.

In modern times *Joseph Andrews* has usually ranked well behind *Tom Jones* in critical esteem. Ian Watt, in his influential study *The Rise of the Novel*, describes *Joseph Andrews* as 'a hurriedly composed work of somewhat mixed intentions'. He, like a number of other recent critics, felt that Fielding was torn between creating a parody of Richardson and an imitation of Cervantes, and that the result, while often charming, was a confused work of fiction. It is Martin Battestin who among all modern critics has done most to enhance this novel's reputation. His insistence on seeing it as a coherent and consistent moral pilgrimage in his book *The Moral Basis of Fielding's Art* has changed the way in which most informed modern readers regard the book. Yet it seems appropriate to conclude with the observations of one of Fielding's contemporaries, whose simple pleasure in the book comes closest to the spirit of Fielding's work. Writing to her friend Catherine Talbot on New Year's day 1743, Elizabeth Carter said of *Joseph Andrews*:

It contains such a surprizing variety of nature, wit, morality, and good sense, as is scarcely to be met with in any one composition, and there is such a spirit of benevolence runs through the whole, as I think renders it peculiarly charming.

Further Reading

EDITIONS The most authoritative, scholarly edition of *Joseph Andrews* available is that included in the new Wesleyan Edition of *The Complete Works of Henry Fielding*, edited by W. B. Coley (Oxford, 1967). However, for practical purposes, the most useful editions for students are these:

Penguin English Library, edited by R. F. Brissenden (1977);
Oxford English Novels, edited by Douglas Brooks (1971);
Riverside Edition (Boston), edited by Martin Battestin (1961).

BIOGRAPHY The most comprehensive biographies of Fielding are *The History of Henry Fielding* (3 vols.) by W. L. Cross (New Haven, 1918) and *Henry Fielding: His Life, Works, and Times* (2 vols.) by F. Homes Dudden (Oxford, 1952).

However, students are likely to find *Henry Fielding* by Pat Rogers (Elek Books, 1979) the most useful and stimulating account of his life and career.

CRITICISM The best single book on *Joseph Andrews* is *The Moral Basis of Fielding's Art* by Martin Battestin (Wesleyan University Press, 1959, 1964). This deals in detail with the moral and religious themes in the novel.

See also Homer Goldberg, *The Art of* Joseph Andrews (University of Chicago Press, 1969).

There is an interesting article on *Joseph Andrews* by Mark Spilka, entitled 'Comic Resolution in Fielding's *Joseph Andrews*', in *College English* (1953), pp. 11–19.

There are a number of critical books on Fielding's writings as a whole which might also prove useful. See, in particular, the following:

R. Alter, *Fielding and the Nature of the Novel* (Cambridge, Mass., 1968);
J. P. Hunter, *Occasional Form: Henry Fielding and the Chains of Circumstance* (Baltimore, 1975);
M. Johnson, *Fielding's Art of Fiction* (Philadelphia, 1961);
R. Paulson (ed.), *Fielding: A Collection of Critical Essays* (Englewood Cliffs, N. J., 1962);
A. Wright, *Henry Fielding: Mask and Feast* (London and Berkeley, 1965).

GENERAL   Two general books which might prove especially useful for students of *Joseph Andrews* are the following:

Ian Watt, *The Rise of the Novel* (Penguin, 1963), the most lively and stimulating account of fictional styles and developments in the early eighteenth century.

Pat Rogers, *The Augustan Vision* (Weidenfeld, 1974), a fascinating introduction to eighteenth-century literature and society.

FOR THE BEST IN PAPERBACKS, LOOK FOR THE

In every corner of the world, on every subject under the sun, Penguins represent quality and variety – the very best in publishing today.

For complete information about books available from Penguin and how to order them, write to us at the appropriate address below. Please note that for copyright reasons the selection of books varies from country to country.

In the United Kingdom: For a complete list of books available from Penguin in the U.K., please write to *Dept EP, Penguin Books Ltd, Harmondsworth, Middlesex, UB7 0DA*

In the United States: For a complete list of books available from Penguin in the U.S., please write to *Dept BA, Viking Penguin, 299 Murray Hill Parkway, East Rutherford, New Jersey 07073*

In Canada: For a complete list of books available from Penguin in Canada, please write to *Penguin Books Canada Limited, 2801 John Street, Markham, Ontario L3R 1B4*

In Australia: For a complete list of books available from Penguin in Australia, please write to the *Marketing Department, Penguin Books Australia Ltd, P.O. Box 257, Ringwood, Victoria 3134*

In New Zealand: For a complete list of books available from Penguin in New Zealand, please write to the *Marketing Department, Penguin Books (N.Z.) Ltd, Private Bag, Takapuna, Auckland 9*

In India: For a complete list of books available from Penguin in India, please write to *Penguin Overseas Ltd, 706 Eros Apartments, 56 Nehru Place, New Delhi 110019*

THE LIBRARY OF EVERY CIVILIZED PERSON

THE LIBRARY OF EVERY CIVILIZED PERSON

Benjamin Disraeli	**Sybil**
George Eliot	**Adam Bede**
	Daniel Deronda
	Felix Holt
	Middlemarch
	The Mill on the Floss
	Romola
	Scenes of Clerical Life
	Silas Marner
Elizabeth Gaskell	**Cranford** and **Cousin Phillis**
	The Life of Charlotte Brontë
	Mary Barton
	North and South
	Wives and Daughters
Edward Gibbon	**The Decline and Fall of the Roman Empire**
George Gissing	**New Grub Street**
Edmund Gosse	**Father and Son**
Richard Jefferies	**Landscape with Figures**
Thomas Macaulay	**The History of England**
Henry Mayhew	**Selections from London Labour** and **The London Poor**
John Stuart Mill	**On Liberty**
William Morris	**News from Nowhere** and **Selected Writings and Designs**
Walter Pater	**Marius the Epicurean**
John Ruskin	**'Unto This Last' and Other Writings**
Sir Walter Scott	**Ivanhoe**
Robert Louis Stevenson	**Dr Jekyll and Mr Hyde**
William Makepeace Thackeray	**The History of Henry Esmond**
	Vanity Fair
Anthony Trollope	**Barchester Towers**
	Framley Parsonage
	Phineas Finn
	The Warden
Mrs Humphrey Ward	**Helbeck of Bannisdale**
Mary Wollstonecraft	**Vindication of the Rights of Women**

FOR THE BEST IN PAPERBACKS, LOOK FOR THE

PENGUIN MODERN CLASSICS

The Collected Stories of Elizabeth Bowen

Seventy-nine stories – love stories, ghost stories, stories of childhood and of London during the Blitz – which all prove that 'the instinctive artist is there at the very heart of her work' – Angus Wilson

Tarr   Wyndham Lewis

A strange picture of a grotesque world where human relationships are just fodder for a master race of artists, Lewis's extraordinary book remains 'a masterpiece of the period' – V. S. Pritchett

Chéri and The Last of Chéri   Colette

Two novels that 'form the classic analysis of a love-affair between a very young man and a middle-aged woman' – Raymond Mortimer

Selected Poems 1923–1967   Jorge Luis Borges

A magnificent bilingual edition of the poetry of one of the greatest writers of today, conjuring up a unique world of invisible roses, uncaught tigers . . .

Beware of Pity   Stefan Zweig

A cavalry officer becomes involved in the suffering of a young girl; when he attempts to avoid the consequences of his behaviour, the results prove fatal . . .

Valmouth and Other Novels   Ronald Firbank

The world of Ronald Firbank – vibrant, colourful and fantastic – is to be found beneath soft deeps of velvet sky dotted with cognac clouds.